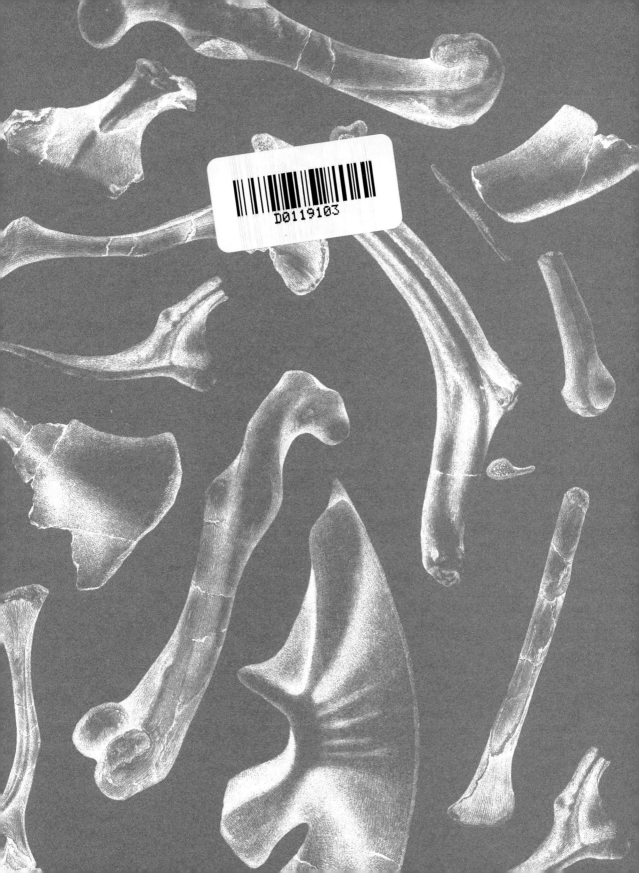

D0119103

THE FIRST DINOSAUR

HOW SCIENCE SOLVED THE GREATEST MYSTERY ON EARTH

IAN LENDLER

ILLUSTRATED BY

C. M. BUTZER

MARGARET K. McELDERRY BOOKS

New York   London   Toronto   Sydney   New Delhi

To Theo, Dylan, and Kusum,
who know more about dinosaurs now
than they ever wanted to.

–I. L.

MARGARET K. McELDERRY BOOKS
An imprint of Simon & Schuster Children's Publishing Division
1230 Avenue of the Americas, New York, New York 10020
Text copyright © 2019 by Ian Lendler
Illustrations copyright © 2019 by C. M. Butzer
All rights reserved, including the right of reproduction in whole or in
part in any form.
MARGARET K. McELDERRY BOOKS is a trademark of Simon &
Schuster, Inc.
For information about special discounts for bulk purchases, please
contact Simon & Schuster Special Sales at 1-866-506-1949 or
business@simonandschuster.com.
The Simon & Schuster Speakers Bureau can bring authors to your live
event. For more information or to book an event, contact the Simon &
Schuster Speakers Bureau at 1-866-248-3049 or visit our website at
www.simonspeakers.com.
Jacket design by Greg Stadnyk
Interior design by Irene Metaxatos and Rebecca Syracuse
The text for this book was set in Fournier Lt Std.
The illustrations for this book were rendered in pen, ink, and digitally.
Manufactured in China
0719 SCP   First Edition   10 9 8 7 6 5 4 3 2 1
CIP data for this book is available from the Library of Congress.
ISBN 978-1-5344-2700-6
ISBN 978-1-5344-2702-0 (eBook)

CONTENTS

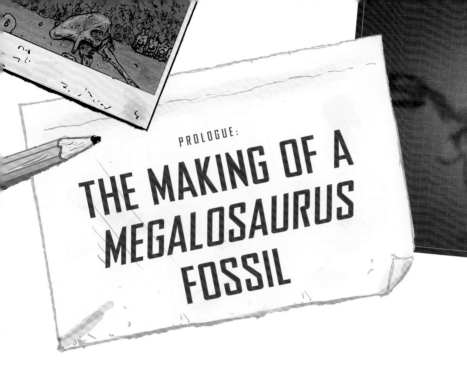

THE MAKING OF A MEGALOSAURUS FOSSIL

168–166 MILLION YEARS AGO
[MIDDLE JURASSIC PERIOD]

There were many ways that a *Megalosaurus* could die.

Maybe it couldn't find enough food, so it starved to death.

Maybe it tried to hunt the wrong food. The mid-Jurassic period was home to some of the largest animals ever to walk on Earth, like the 90-foot-long *Diplodocus*. Its 45-foot tail could swing with enough speed to crack the air like a whip and kill a smaller animal such as *Megalosaurus*.

Or maybe the megalosaur just died from plain old bad luck. It stepped in a hole and broke its ankle. Or a tree fell on its head.

In the wild, death from old age isn't an option. Life is nasty, brutish, and short.

No matter how it happened, the body sank down into the mud. Insects and scavengers quickly stripped away the skin and meat, leaving nothing behind but the bones.

Over millions of years, it was joined by its brothers, sisters, cousins, and great-great-grandchildren. The mud covered all of them in one giant, unmarked grave. Then slowly, slowly the minerals began to leach into the bones, turning them to stone.

They became fossils.

161–145 MILLION YEARS AGO
[LATE JURASSIC PERIOD]

The Earth's surface is grinding together. The continents are breaking apart. The fossil bones begin to move.

Ocean waters rush in over the grave of the megalosaurs. The mineral-rich water

soaks into the bones, coating them in tiny bits of coral and shell.

Tides come and go, sweeping more mud over the grave. The weight of the water and the mud crushes down, forming a solid layer of rock known as limestone. The bones are no longer buried in mud. Now, they are encased in a coffin of hard rock.

65 MILLION YEARS AGO
(K-T EXTINCTION EVENT)

A light tremor in the ground rattles the bones.

It doesn't feel like much, but on the other side of the planet (in what will later become Mexico), Death has arrived.

It comes in the form of a comet approximately seven miles wide that slams into Earth at a speed of 10 miles per second. The explosion vaporizes three-quarters of all life on Earth. Everything on the planet's surface turns to ash.

Around the entire planet, that ash forms a thin layer known as the K-T boundary. That boundary is a coffin lid closing over the entire era of large dinosaurs. No dinosaur bone will ever be found above that boundary line.

All traces of *Megalosaurus* and its kind are wiped clean from the surface of the planet.

Oxfordshire, England. A county full of mining villages totally unaware of what lay beneath their feet.

65–23 MILLION YEARS AGO
(PALEOGENE PERIOD)

Volcanic eruptions, earthquakes, and receding oceans push the tomb of the megalosaurs up out of the water. Around the tomb is a piece of land big enough to be called an island.

It will be another 20 million years before the first humans evolve and start their funny habit of naming things. But when then do, they will name this island "Pretani" ("tattooed people") to describe the earliest people who lived there.

That word soon changes into what we know today as "Britain."

And there, in an area of Britain known as Oxfordshire, the bones waited. They waited for someone with a hammer and chisel to pull them out—one by one—from their grave. But to put those pieces back together, to re-form *Megalosaurus*, required a tool far more powerful than a hammer and chisel.

It required an idea.

IMAGINE . . .

Try to imagine a *Megalosaurus*.

A 10-foot-tall, 30-foot-long, meat-eating reptile that weighed between 3,000 and 7,000 pounds. Its jaws had 3-inch, razor-sharp teeth that could tear 100 pounds of flesh off its victim in one bite.

Actually, that isn't so hard, is it? Everyone can picture dozens of different dinosaurs in their head. We learn about dinosaurs when we're very young and we accept the idea because, at that age, our imagination is open to anything. Plus, giant reptiles are awesome.

As we grow, the idea of dinosaurs is reinforced through movies, TV shows, video games, toys, and books. Dinosaurs have become a permanent part of our culture.

Now try to imagine this:

You're living 200 years ago. At that point, humans had no idea that dinosaurs existed. There were no dinosaur books, dinosaur toys, or dinosaur movies. Many people didn't even think Earth existed before the appearance of human beings.

Now imagine trying to explain *Megalosaurus* to that version of you. Or explain an *Ankylosaurus*—a 4-ton, 6-foot tall, 20-foot-long, plant-eating reptile that's covered with spikes made of bone. It basically sounds insane.

Now, in that frame of mind, imagine you were one of the quarry workers in Oxfordshire, England, in 1676 who came across a rather oddly shaped rock that looked the bone shown on the left.

This is the first dinosaur fossil ever pictured. It was like finding one piece of a jigsaw puzzle, and trying to rebuild the entire puzzle without seeing the picture on the box. Or knowing there was even a puzzle to solve.

It was only in 1824 that scientists realized that it was most likely the thighbone of a *Megalosaurus*—the first dinosaur ever discovered.

What happened in the 200 years between the discovery of the first bone and the first dinosaur that helped humans piece together the puzzle? How did we discover the *idea* of dinosaurs?

How did we imagine (and prove) the existence of something that we cannot see?

This is *Megalosaurus*—the first dinosaur ever discovered.

PART I

TOUCHING THE ELEPHANT

THE SIX BLIND MEN AND THE ELEPHANT

Once, an elephant wandered into a village. In this village lived six blind men who had no idea what an elephant was. So they all visited the elephant and placed their hands on it to feel for themselves.

The first blind man felt the trunk and said, "I see. An elephant is like a snake."

The second blind man felt the leg and said, "No. An elephant is like a tree."

The third blind man felt the ear and said, "It's like a large fan."

The fourth blind man felt the side and said, "It's a massive wall."

The fifth blind man felt the tusk and said, "It's a sharp spear."

The sixth blind man felt the tail and said, "You're all wrong. An elephant is a type of rope."

They began to argue over who was right when someone walking by overheard them. He told them, "You are all wrong. But you are also all right. You only touched one part of the whole thing."

This book is the story of a group of naturalists, philosophers, hobbyists, and scientists who were blindly searching underground when they touched an "elephant."

This is the story of how they saw the light.

THE FIRST BONE
1676, OXFORDSHIRE, ENGLAND

The bone was from an elephant. It had to be.

At least, that's the only thing Dr. Plot could think of as he studied the large fossilized bone in his hand (pictured left). Workers at a local quarry had found it 60 feet underground and called him to investigate.

His nickname was "the learned Dr. Plot" because he was the expert on all plant and animal life around Oxford, the oldest university in England. So he knew there was no animal in the entire country—not even an ox—that was big enough to produce a bone like this. Actually, it was only a *fragment* of a bone, but it still measured 2 feet long and weighed 20 pounds!

Dr. Plot had never actually seen an elephant, mind you. The only people in seventeenth-century England lucky enough to see an elephant were those who had access to the king's personal zoo in the Tower of London. But the *idea* of elephants in England was famous.

Every schoolchild knew the story of how the Romans conquered Britain. The Roman emperor, Caesar, attacked the island in 55 B.C., but was pushed back by fierce local tribes. So Caesar returned a year later with the Roman army's most terrifying weapon—a war elephant.

The Romans took a 10,000-pound, 10-foot-tall African elephant and covered it in iron armor. They mounted a squad of archers on its back, whipped the animal into a frenzy, and sent it charging into battle. The Britons had never seen anything like it. A Roman historian gleefully described what happened next: "If the Britons were terrified at so extraordinary a spectacle, what shall I say of their

Roman war elephant causing carnage in battle.

horses? The Britons . . . abandoned themselves to flight, leaving the Romans to pass the river unmolested, after the enemy had been routed by the appearance of a single beast."

The bone in Plot's hand was certainly old enough to come from that original war elephant. It had been buried so long that it had somehow mysteriously turned to stone.

In reality, Plot was holding the first *Megalosaurus* bone ever discovered, but he didn't know that. In the seventeenth century, very little was known about fossils in general and absolutely no one had any idea that dinosaurs existed. Beneath the surface of Earth was an unknown, alien world filled with mystery.

THE MYSTERY OF THE FORMED STONES

The word "fossil" didn't mean what it does today.

A "fossil" in Plot's time meant "anything dug up from the ground." That applied to everything from pottery and coins to rocks, crystals, and the most peculiar thing of all, "formed stones." These were the stone objects pulled out of the ground that looked exactly like plants, shells, and bones.

Nowadays, we know that these fossils are the mineralized remains of ancient animal and plant life. But people in the seventeenth century were baffled. They had no idea what they were, where they came from, or how they were made.

They did, however, have a lot of theories.

> **"Mystery creates wonder and wonder is the basis of man's desire to understand."**
> —NEIL ARMSTRONG

One of the most popular ideas was that there was a "plastic force" in the ground. Earth (although some said it was a "World Soul" or a "Realm of Eternal Forms") was jealous of the world aboveground and used this "plastic force" to twist itself into copies of living things.

Others believed that formed stones were caused by the stars and moon exerting cosmic forces upon Earth. Some believed that fossils were like flowers that grew underground—they were nature's way of making the underworld more beautiful. Or better yet, fossils were simply funny coincidences, or "sports of nature," in which stones came to look like bones.

In the local quarries, Dr. Plot frequently found "formed stones" that looked like seashells and fish skeletons. As a professor of chemistry at Oxford University, he tried to come up with more "scientific" explanations for their existence. Perhaps, he thought, the "plastic force" was not some spiritual force but simply salt (and urine!) crystals, which grew into these shapes by pure coincidence.

However, this larger bone was different. Plot had to admit that it looked *so* similar to an animal bone that it couldn't just be crystals. It must have come from an *actual* animal.

As he struggled with how to identify the bone, Plot had a stroke of luck. "There happily came to Oxford . . . a living Elephant to be shown publicly."

An elephant in England! This was a rare treat indeed. The general public saw it as grand entertainment. Dr. Plot saw it as an opportunity for research. He compared his mystery bone against the elephant. What he found surprised him: "Those [bones] of the Elephant were not only of a different Shape, but also incomparably bigger than ours. . . ."

Dr. Plot was stumped. In desperation (or in search of inspiration), he looked in the Bible and read:

"There were giants in the earth . . ."

—Genesis 6:4

In the book of Deuteronomy is the story of a king named Og, who was 12 feet tall, and "a land of giants" who were "the height of the cedars and . . . as strong as the oaks."

In seventeenth-century Europe, the Bible was seen as the ultimate source of truth. This was all the proof that Plot needed. He wrote about his fossil: "If then they are neither the Bones of Horses, Oxen, nor Elephants . . . they must have been the bones of Men or Women."

Plot wasn't the first person to turn to religion to explain the existence of fossils. For tens of thousands of years, humans told stories and invented mythologies to explain things about the world that they didn't understand—rain, thunder, lightning. And two of the biggest mysteries of all were the stars in the sky above and the bones in the ground below.

What's fascinating is that in cultures around the world (even though they were separated by oceans and thousands of miles), these stories wound up sounding similar. When early humans looked up at the stars, they saw gods. When they looked at the massive bones in the ground, they saw monsters.

GODS AND MONSTERS

It was a modern folklorist named Adrienne Mayor who first noticed that the ancient Greek stories of the griffin (which had the body of a lion, head and claws of an eagle, tail of a serpent) perfectly described a *Protoceratops*. The Greeks believed that the griffin guarded treasures of gold. Mayor discovered that fossilized skulls of *Protoceratops* were often found in Mongolia, where the Greeks traveled to trade for gold.

Once Mayor made this connection, many stories from ancient religions made sense. Skulls of extinct mastodons, a common sight in Greece, were imagined as a race of one-eyed giants called Cyclops.

There were similar stories all around the world. In North America, many Native American tribes had myths that tried to explain the origins of fossils. The Sioux tribe of the South Dakota badlands believed in "Unktehi," a mythical, horned, water-monster god, which closely matches the description of the recently discovered *Dracorex hogwartsia* (yes, its name is inspired by Harry Potter).

In Mexico, the Mayans believed the god of the underworld was a giant crocodile. Cliffs and caves around the sites of Mayan cities show large numbers of crocodile and fish teeth fossilized into the rocks. In China, farmers dug up massive, fang-filled reptile skulls and imagined a race of ancient dragons. In each case, these monsters had mysteriously vanished from Earth.

These stories show that humans have had a long and deep fascination with fossils and the idea that we shared the same planet with other, more exotic forms of life. But none of them helped to solve the mystery of what these creatures truly were, where they had come from, or where they had gone.

Myths have the same problem as the theories of plastic and crystalized pee. None of them are based on evidence. Since a myth contains no specific information (measurements, data), it's impossible to prove or disprove. It's impossible for others to examine and develop their own ideas.

This left every fossil open to whatever interpretation someone wanted to give. For instance, a century after Plot decided his fossil was the thighbone of a biblical giant, a physician named Richard Brookes examined the same bone and came to a slightly different conclusion.

To him, it looked exactly like a pair of giant testicles. He named it accordingly: "*Scrotum humanum.*"

WHERE WE BEGIN

Humans have been wondering over fossils for thousands of years, but the reason this book starts with this particular fossil is because of what Dr. Plot did next.

He examined it closely. He measured and described it in detail (weight, size, composition). He even illustrated it . . . *and then he recorded all*

A DINOSAUR NAMED SCROTUM

When it comes to naming a species, there are a number of very precise rules and regulations. One of them goes something like this: If a fossil is discovered and given a name, and then turns out to be part of a unique species, then that species should take the name of that first fossil.

In the 1970s, a paleontologist (perhaps jokingly) argued that by this logic, Megalosaurus should have its name changed to scrotum humanum (or perhaps scrotum-o-saurus, for short).

To decide the matter, an international panel of experts sat around in a room and seriously debated the pros and cons of renaming the first dinosaur in history after a large testicle. They decided against it.

The Megalosaurus name survived.

of this information in a book.

Plot may not have understood fossils, but *because* of this record we are able to look back and identify what it truly was—the thighbone of a megalosaur.

Plot had created the first scientific illustration and description of a dinosaur bone.

He didn't come up with this idea on his own. It was one of the fundamental techniques of a new method of thinking that was spreading all over Europe at the time. Its name was Science, and it was the key to unraveling the mystery of "the formed stones."

Despite his efforts, Plot couldn't really be considered a "scientist" from a modern perspective (the word itself wouldn't even be invented for another 150 years). His ideas were still rooted in the world of plastics, crystals, and monsters from the Bible.

Ironically, the transition away from mystery and mythology to scientific fact truly began when two fishermen pulled a real-life monster from the sea.

Since science begins with the gathering and recording of information, then the science of dinosaurs began with this book.

Fig: 5

Fig: 6.

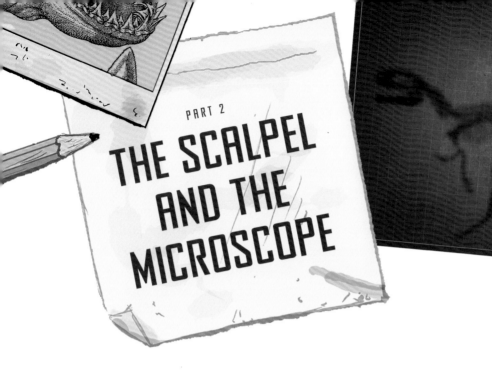

PART 2
THE SCALPEL AND THE MICROSCOPE

THE MONSTER FROM THE DEEP
1666

The Mediterranean Sea is one of the most beautiful places in the world, but when two French fishermen lowered their hooks beneath the brilliant blue surface of the water, they had no idea that there were monsters lurking below.

Now they were in a fight for their lives. Something bit their line, and it was large enough and strong enough to drag their boat for miles or destroy it. They didn't have time to sail home. They had to land immediately, so they made for the nearest shore, which happened to be in Italy.

As they approached, the local villagers ran out to lend a hand. Working together, they dragged the fish out of the water. Even on dry land, it thrashed so violently they had to stop it before it killed someone. So they lashed it to a tree and beat it with clubs until it was dead. Only then could they get a proper look at it.

It was a great white shark—2,800 pounds of pure muscle.

The news spread fast. Great whites were a rare catch in the Mediterranean Sea, and a beast of that size was the catch of a lifetime. The story traveled from village to village until it made its way to the nearest city, Florence. The Grand Duke who ruled Florence was so impressed that he called for the beast to be brought to the capital so he could see it in person.

This was easier said than done. Florence was 60 miles away. The shark was so large that there was no way they could carry its body that far. So they came up with a solution. They chopped off the head of the shark and loaded it onto the back of a cart.

Whoever they passed along the way would have experienced the strangest sight (and worst smell) of their life—the massive, rotting head of a great white shark resting on the back of a horse-drawn cart, slowly creaking its way up a dirt road toward one of the most extraordinary places on Earth—Florence, Italy.

If those fishermen had landed in any other country, near any other city, that shark would have simply become a local fishing legend, a trophy, or soup. But Florence was different.

Florence is the city where Science was born.

THE CITY OF REVOLUTION

The fishermen were driving the shark head into a city in the middle of a revolution. But there was no blood on the streets, no angry mobs carrying pitchforks. Instead, they passed students carrying books. They passed students setting up exotic new technologies like thermometers, barometers, and

Galileo Galilei,
Godfather of science.

weather gauges around the city. The students belonged to the Accademia del Cimento ("school of experiments"). This was the very first school dedicated to the idea of measurements and experimentation. It was also where the first piece of the puzzle of dinosaurs would fall into place.

It seems strange, from our modern perspective, to think of "science" as an invention, but that's what it is. Science is a tool created by humans to discover the truth about the world around them. Without it, the discovery of dinosaurs would have been impossible.

This was the Scientific Revolution.

There are many reasons why the Scientific Revolution occurred:

- The invention of the printing press in the fifteenth century spread ideas further and faster than ever before.

- The rise of the Protestant religion in the sixteenth century challenged the idea that the Catholic Church was the only source of knowledge.

- The invention of mechanical clocks (in the fourteenth century in Europe, although it was much earlier in China) showed that time—the rhythm of the sun and moon—could be measured and copied.

- The invention of the telescope in 1608 showed that the planets and stars followed the same patterns as the sun.

Galileo observing the night sky with students in Venice, Italy.

From this, philosophers came to a realization. A clock is a machine—a collection of moving parts that follows simple rules. If a machine can mimic the movements of the universe, then maybe the universe itself is just one big machine. *Maybe the universe follows a few simple rules.*

Science began with the idea that if we take enough measurements, and analyze them correctly, we can figure out the rules of the universe. Florence became the first city (with the first school) dedicated to this idea because it was the home of one of the first, and most important, scientific revolutionaries—Galileo Galilei.

THE TRUTH IS IN THE STARS

It's one of the peculiar quirks of science that the solution to the mystery of bones in the ground began when humans looked up in the sky.

Galileo Galilei (1564–1642) was a clock maker, inventor, engineer, and mathematician. But perhaps his greatest contribution to science was his study of space. Excited by the invention of telescopes, Galileo built (by hand) the most powerful telescope of the time. He used it to observe and precisely record the movements of the planets and stars. Then, he mathematically proved that Earth revolved around the sun.

That directly contradicted the Catholic Church, which taught that the universe revolved around Earth. To silence him, the church sentenced Galileo to permanent house arrest at his home in Florence. But that didn't stop Galileo.

Since Galileo couldn't leave his house, he invited people in. He turned his home into a school for a whole new generation of students, including Ferdinand de' Medici, the young prince of Florence. When Ferdinand became the Grand Duke, he created the "school of experiments" in 1657. It was dedicated to following Galileo's advice:

4. Test your hypothesis with an experiment
5. Reach a conclusion: accept or reject your hypothesis

This became known as the Scientific Method, and the professors and students

> "We ought to begin not with Scriptures, but with experimentation and demonstration."
>
> —GALILEO GALILEI

Galileo stressed the importance of observation. This may seem obvious, but the idea of "observing the world around you" was relatively new. Before the creation of science, many European scholars believed that all human knowledge was contained in a few books, such as the Holy Bible. Learning meant memorizing those books, and obeying the teachings of the Catholic Church. Discovering new ideas outside those books wasn't just wrong, it went against the word of God.

Galileo disagreed and helped develop a series of steps for discovering the truth:

1. Observe
2. Ask a question
3. Create an explanation for your question (a "hypothesis")

of the Accademia del Cimento were the first to use it. As the success of the school grew, different buildings were

Galileo is punk

Galileo could easily have avoided his punishment. When he published his findings in the book *Starry Messenger* (1610), the church put him on trial for heresy (contradicting the teachings of the church).

They found him guilty, but the pope set him free with only one demand—that Galileo stop teaching. Galileo, however, was not the sort of person who liked being told what to do. He wrote another book with a character based on the pope. The pope character's name was "Simpleton."

The pope was not amused. He banned *Starry Messenger* and arrested Galileo.

established around Florence to explore different areas of science.

It was one of these buildings that was the final destination of the fishermen and their cart. When they pulled up in front of the school, several men were required to lift the stinking, rotting shark head off the cart and carry it inside. There, they placed it on a table specially set up in the middle of a stage. Waiting for them was a 27-year-old man with shoulder-length black hair by the name of Nicolaus Steno.

Next to the table was a set of knives that Steno began to sharpen. It was time for his show to begin. . . .

THE SCALPEL

The Scientific Revolution spun off into many different subjects—physics, astronomy, zoology, chemistry. But the most popular by far was anatomy.

The idea of dissecting a human body to understand how it works started with the ancient Greeks. But when the Catholic Church rose to power, it condemned the practice as blasphemous. Doctors wanting to learn about the human body weren't allowed to study an actual human body. Instead, they had to memorize a book written by one of the Greeks (1,500 years earlier) about the internal organs of an ape.

This changed in the seventeenth cen-tury when a group of French medical students, inspired by the ideas of the Scientific Revolution, began sneaking into cemeteries at night. They stole the bodies of executed criminals, dissected them in secret, then wrote and illustrated books detailing what they found. These images proved so helpful to doctors that the church relented and allowed the dissection of cadavers to continue.

The popularity of dissection skyrocketed. "Anatomy theaters" were built to hold large crowds. Tickets were sold to the general public, who came to see bodies opened and to touch the internal organs that were passed around. To make extra money, anatomy professors made belts from the cadavers' skin and sold them as souvenirs after the show.

Of all the anatomists in Europe, the most famous was Nicolaus Steno. His talent for dissection was obvious from the moment he entered medical school in his home country of Denmark.

"In truth, he is a genius," wrote one of his teachers. His skills with a knife were extraordinary, but what made him truly stand out were his observational skills.

Up until that time, people thought the human heart was a boiling pot of blood or a container that held the "vapors" of our

One of the earliest anatomy theaters (17th century). Leiden University, Netherlands. Note the social atmosphere.

soul. Steno's knife laid bare the truth—the heart was a plain old muscle.

He discovered the salivary gland and the tear gland. Before this, people thought that tears were caused by grief literally squeezing fluid out of the brain. Steno wrote several books about his discoveries, which proved surprisingly popular. The excitement of the Scientific Revolution was slowly spreading out beyond a small group of "natural historians," as early scientists were called, and into the educated public.

Steno took advantage of this to earn a living. He left school and began touring the capitals of Europe like a rock star. He visited wealthy homes and provided after-dinner entertainment at parties. As well-dressed ladies and gentlemen gathered around, he would dissect sheep heads and horse eyeballs and explain the latest research.

One partygoer wrote,

"This Monsieur Steno is the rage here [in Paris]. . . . Neither a butterfly nor a fly escapes his skill. He would count the bones of a flea—if a flea had bones."

Word of Steno's skills eventually reached Grand Duke Ferdinand in Florence, who invited him to the Accademia. That is how Steno found himself standing onstage next to a giant shark's head as the members of the Accademia—philosophers, naturalists, and inventors—filed into the theater. The Grand Duke was there, eager to see Steno perform.

When they had taken their seats, Steno approached the shark. The whole audience would have leaned forward eagerly to get a better view. Then Steno picked up his knife . . . and sliced open the head.

In the tradition of Galileo, he began to observe.

He found the shark's ear, hidden underneath the skin. He noted the surprisingly small size of its brain (only 3 ounces). But it was the jaws that truly caught his attention. They were large enough to swallow a grown man. And those teeth . . .

They were 3 inches long and razor sharp. There were thirteen *rows* of them, lined up and ready to replace any that broke off while chewing a particularly tasty treat. More importantly, Steno couldn't help but notice that he had seen teeth like these before. They looked exactly like *glossopetrae*—also known as tongue-stones.

Steno's patient and costar on the anatomy stage, 1667.

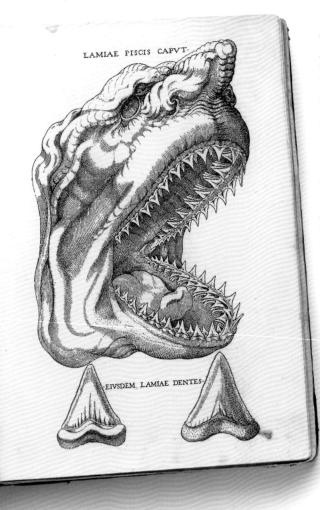

BONE, NOT STONE

Tongue-stones were small, triangular pieces of stone that supposedly looked like the tongue of a dragon. They were very popular in Italy at the time and many people wore them as good luck charms around their neck. This "good luck" came in many forms. People believed that tongue-stones could guard against liquid poison and sorcerers' spells. They could heal "plagues, ill-disposed fevers, burns, poxes, pustules," as well as labor pains and epilepsy. If a young man wanted to "court faire women," they were "very necessary," possibly because they could also prevent bad breath.

The supposed healing power of tongue-stones was so remarkable that their legend had reached as far north as Denmark, where Steno studied them in medical school. Despite their popularity, tongue-stones were surrounded in mystery. They mostly came from Malta, an island off the coast of Italy, where *tens* of thousands of them were embedded in the cliffs (or sometimes simply lying on the ground). What they were and how they got there, no one had any idea.

It was a mystery that many had tried to solve. Two thousand years earlier, the Greek philosopher Aristotle thought they looked like fish teeth. This guess was entirely correct, but there was no scientific method at the time to help separate fact from fiction. And there was plenty of fiction.

Another Greek philosopher, named Pliny the Elder, believed that since you could find tongue-stones on the ground, they must have fallen from the skies like rain. No one had actually *seen* this happen, so Pliny decided they must have fallen only on moonless nights.

A different explanation was taken from the Bible. In one story, the apostle Paul was shipwrecked on Malta. As he gathered wood to build a fire, a deadly viper lunged out and bit him. Paul merely shook the snake loose and carried on unharmed. He did, however, curse the viper so that it would no longer have teeth. The locals believed that Mother Nature celebrated this moment by growing viper-tooth-shaped stones on the island (although in

For a sense of megalodon's massive size, compare the shark tooth (in white) to the *Megalosaurus* tooth underneath.

truth, tongue-stones look nothing like viper fangs).

Not everyone believed these popular explanations. "Nobody is so stupid . . . ," wrote a man named Fabio Colonna. A few years before Steno, he had taken it upon himself to investigate tongue-stones as a possible cure for his epilepsy. He concluded, "The teeth are of the nature of bones, not stones."

Nowadays, we know that tongue-stones came from megalodon, a terrifyingly large, 60-foot, prehistoric shark that lived 16 to 2 million years ago. But no one in Florence had ever seen teeth of that size before since sharks are notoriously shy about going to the dentist.

Staring into the massive jaws of the shark on the dissection table, Steno had a view that very few people ever got to see . . . and lived to tell about it. To Steno, the evidence seemed clear as day.

He observed: "The shape of the tongue-stones is like shark teeth."

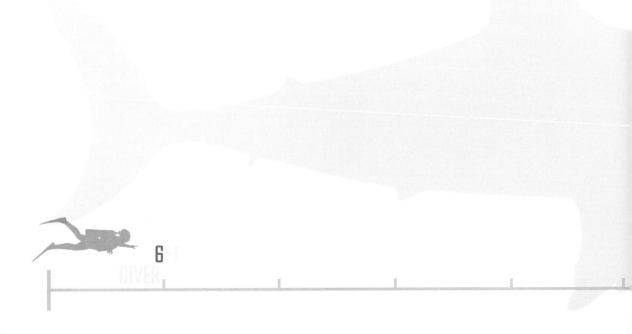

He measured: "They are quite alike, planes to planes, sides to sides, base to base. . . ."

He concluded: "That [tongue-stones] are shark's teeth is proved by their shape."

In 1667, Steno published his observations in the fantastically titled book *A Shark's Head Dissected*. The book's main focus was on the shark's anatomy. His observations on tongue-stones, which became one of his most important contributions to science, were shoved into a subsection.

It may not seem obvious, but Steno had taken the first step in uncovering the mystery of dinosaurs. He had figured out the "what."

"What are fossils?"

They are the remains of old animals and plants. Other people had made the connection before, but by directly comparing and measuring the fossil and modern teeth, Steno could prove it.

The next step was figuring out the "how." How did fossils get under the ground? How did they turn from bone to stone?

Steno became fascinated with that question. He became so obsessed with the origin of tongue-stones that he quit his anatomy work so he could travel to

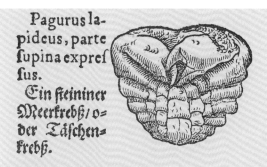

The First Fossil

In 1565, a Swiss biologist named Conrad Gessner wrote a short but groundbreaking book called *A Book on Fossil Objects, Chiefly Stones and Gems, Their Shapes and Appearances*. This became the first book in which a connection was noted between fossils like this crab pictured above and living creatures.

This was also the first publication that used illustrations of its specimens, making these the first images of a fossil in history. (Fun fact: The book also included the first picture of a pencil!)

Gessner might have gone on to make a stronger connection between fossils and living creatures. He intended to turn his book into a much larger work, but before he could do that he died of plague, in 1565.

their source on the island of Malta. That's where he had a breakthrough that would change the history of Earth.

But while he was doing that, the "how" was being solved on the other side of Europe by the man officially known as "the first scientist in history."

THE FIRST LINK

It's worth restating the fact that others had made the same observations earlier than Steno. But there's a reason that many histories of dinosaurs begin with him—namely, he wrote it down.

Even before Dr. Plot, Steno performed one of the most important acts in the practice of science—he recorded all of his observations and measurements. By doing this, humans only need to discover something once. By recording that discovery, we retain that knowledge and pass it along. Every scientist who comes later can build on top of those preexisting discoveries and ideas.

When Steno published his observations on the shark's anatomy, he became the first link in the chain of ideas that led up to the discovery of dinosaurs.

THE FIRST SCIENTIST

If dinosaurs could not be discovered until humans invented science, and science is a tool, then we needed someone to use that tool. We needed scientists.

The word "scientist" wasn't created until 1834, but the man widely regarded as the first person to work in a laboratory, creating and running experiments, was an incredibly gifted but strange man by the name of Robert Hooke. During his career, he made many valuable contributions to science. Among them were two vital pieces of the dinosaur puzzle. Or more, if you believed him.

When Hooke read Steno's *A Shark's Head Dissected*, he thought Steno's ideas on fossils were so good—*so* brilliant—that Steno had stolen them. From him.

Despite his importance to the history of science, Hooke isn't remembered much today. Possibly because he was considered "the most ill-natured and conceited man in the world." Even his biographer described him as "despicable, being very crooked."

The "crooked" part actually referred to an inherited physical defect that gave him some type of hunched appearance. However, no one quite knows what Hooke looked like.

He was a well-known figure in

he earned admission to the oldest and most prestigious school in England—Oxford University. In 1660, several of his professors decided to form a British version of the Accademia del Cimento in Florence. They called it the "Royal Society of London for the Improving of Natural Knowledge" (or "Royal Society," for short). It is still active today, making it the oldest scientific organization in the world (see next page).

Back then, the only people who had enough leisure time to dabble in science were the rich and aristocratic. They were intellectually fascinated with the idea of experiments, but physically, they didn't really know what they were doing. They needed someone to do the manual labor of running their experiments.

Hooke was not an aristocrat. He was the deformed son of a clergyman from a small, rural island. He may have annoyed people with his arrogance, but he had earned his place at Oxford through his extraordinary mechanical skill. By the age of 13, he had already built by hand a working clock made out of wood, and a model warship with cannons that actually fired.

Despite his intelligence, he was constantly reminded of his place in the social pecking order. He paid his way through Oxford by working as a butler, but he

England so there were very probably paintings of him, but then Hooke picked a fight with Sir Isaac Newton. After Newton was given credit for discovering gravity, Hooke claimed that Newton stole his ideas. (You may notice a pattern by now.) Newton didn't appreciate this, so he used his influence to have every painting of Hooke removed and destroyed. (Moral of the story: It is not a good idea to mess with Sir Isaac Newton.)

Whatever Hooke lacked in people skills, he made up for with his mechanical ability. The Scientific Revolution created a boom in inventions, not just clocks and telescopes, but the microscope, mechanical pump, air gauges, wind gauges, and thermometers. Hooke was able to build, fix, and improve them all. There were several devices that no one else in England could operate except him.

Hooke's talents were so obvious that

never actually graduated. His mechanical skills were so in demand that the Royal Society hired him to be their "curator of experiments." Thus, he became the first person in history to be paid to do scientific research.

His favorite research tool was the microscope. It had been invented 60 years earlier, but Hooke completely redesigned it to improve its power and clarity.

It went from being a simple tube to a complex instrument with multiple parts.

When he finished, he peered into his new and improved microscope and was rewarded with a sight that no human being had ever seen before—a fly's head.

It's hard to imagine the excitement Hooke must have felt in his lab that day. He might as well have been the first man on the moon. He was the *first human in history* to peer into this unknown, microscopic world. He went wild, putting everything he could think of under his microscope lens. The weirder, the better: a piece of moss, leeches in vinegar, fleas, diamonds, a spider's eye, even a chunk of frozen pee(!).

He had studied to be an artist early in his career, so he got out his pen and notepad and began to sketch everything he saw. Science, however, is not always

Sketch of the first compound microscope. Early 17th century.

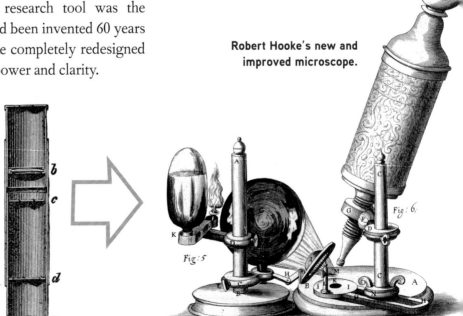

Robert Hooke's new and improved microscope.

easy. For instance, an ant proved impossible to sketch because it kept trying to crawl away (which seems fairly reasonable on the ant's part).

Hooke solved the problem by dosing the ant with brandy, which "knocked [the ant] down dead drunk, so that he became moveless." Hooke made his sketch and, an hour later, the ant woke up and crawled away, presumably with a terrible headache.

In 1665, he published his work in a book titled *Micrographia*. The subtitle explained it a bit better: *Physiological Descriptions of Minute Bodies Made by Magnifying Glasses*. The reaction was immediate.

The publication of *Micrographia* was a turning point in the history of science. In the seventeenth century, very few people understood or even cared about this newfangled "science." Early scien-

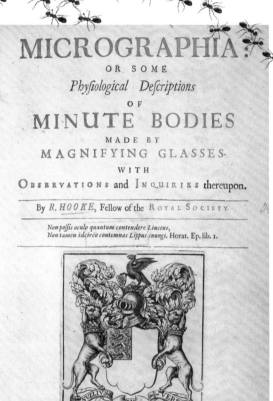

MICROGRAPHIA:
OR SOME
Physiological Descriptions
OF
MINUTE BODIES
MADE BY
MAGNIFYING GLASSES.
WITH
OBSERVATIONS and INQUIRIES thereupon.

By R. HOOKE, Fellow of the ROYAL SOCIETY.

Non possis oculo quantum contendere Linceus,
Non tamen idcirco contemnas Lippus inungi. Horat. Ep. lib. 1.

LONDON, Printed by *Jo. Martyn*, and *Ja. Allestry*, Printers to the
ROYAL SOCIETY, and are to be sold at their Shop at the *Bell* in
S. *Paul's* Church-yard. M DC LX V.

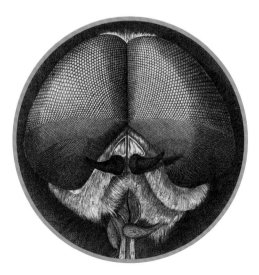

tists were seen as a collection of cranks and oddballs. *Micrographia* changed that. It showed that the methods and ideas of science were able to reveal entire worlds that were previously hidden from view. The book became an instant best seller. It wasn't just a bunch of pretty pictures,

"Before I went to bed I sat up till two o'clock in my chamber reading of Mr. Hooke's [*Micrographia*], the most ingenious book that ever I read in my life."

—SAMUEL PEPYS, SEVENTEENTH-CENTURY WRITER AND POLITICIAN

though. Hooke used what he observed to better understand the world. He looked at a piece of cork . . .

or monk's cell. To this day, when we talk about blood "cells" or plant "cells," we get that word from Hooke.

More importantly (for the discovery of dinosaurs), Hooke examined a slice of fossilized wood . . .

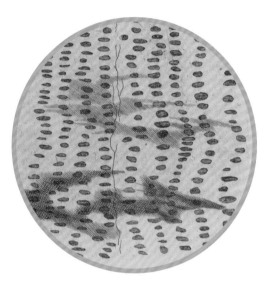

. . . and wrote that it looked exactly like a piece of normal wood, except inside its cells were tiny mineral grains (those dark dots). He concluded that "formed stones" were simply objects from the natural world like bones and plants that had absorbed "petrifying juices" (water filled with minerals).

On one level, Hooke was merely confirming what Steno had guessed. But Hooke was adding an important layer by showing "how" fossilization worked. Some members of the Royal Society were so excited that they got carried away. One member quickly morphed into a mad sci-

. . . and wrote that it was made from small squares that resembled a prisoner's

entist: "If it lay in the power of human skill to raise Petrifaction [an old term for fossilization] or . . . order and direct it, much use might be made of this Art."

Unfortunately, that member left no notes behind detailing what, exactly, he planned to do with the awesome powers of "petrifaction." Another very well-respected naturalist declared that "petrifying juices" were such a strong force that "a whole village in Africa turned into stone, with all the people." He did not back up this claim with any evidence, but you have to love the enthusiasm.

Not everyone agreed with Hooke and Steno. The Royal Society had begun publishing a journal of its lectures to share among its members. The *very first* letter to the editor in the journal's history rejected Hooke's ideas. The author, a prominent naturalist, declared that the idea of petrified shells may be fine for Italy, "but for our *English* inland Quar-

ries which also abound with infinite number and great variety of shells, I am apt to think, that there is no such matter as Petrifying of Shells in the business."

Although ultimately wrong, the author of this letter brought up a very interesting point. All of Steno's discoveries were based on teeth and shells from what we call the Pliocene era (approximately 5 to 2 million years ago, although no one had any idea about this timescale back then). In "geological time" (the lifespan of Earth), that is pretty recent, so a lot of the fossils from that time *look* like creatures that are currently alive. Paleontologists sometimes refer to these as "easy fossils," because they are easy to compare to living species.

However, England's geology was completely different from Italy's. In the rock quarries of England, workers were digging into rocks from the Jurassic period (140 to 200 million ago). This

⸱ ⸱

Birth of the Nerd

When the idea of "the scientist" (or "natural philosopher," as they were known) was born, many countries instantly recognized the military and medical value of this function. Even the Catholic Church created a whole department for scientific research.

English culture, however, took a different approach. King Charles referred to the members of the Royal Society as "my ferrets." A visiting Italian scientist reacted with pity when he saw how an English scientist was treated at a party: "The ladies at once believe that he must be enamored of the moon, or Venus, or some silly thing like that."

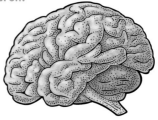

Ammonite from Yorkshire, UK.

meant they were uncovering fossils like the ammonites.

Ammonites were early shell-dwelling cousins of squid, and during the Jurassic period they were one of the most numerous species on Earth. Their distinctive coiled shells were found in massive numbers all over England. They could be as small as a fingernail or as large as a wagon wheel, sometimes clumped together in the hundreds. Because of their coiled appearance, locals believed that they were snakes that had turned to stone. They treated them much like tongue-stones, and kept them as good luck charms.

Ammonites were greatly admired because they were so exotic. They don't look like any other living creature on Earth. That's because unbeknownst to people at the time, the ammonite had gone extinct 65 million years ago. No one understood this back then because they were missing one crucial piece of information.

They had no idea that animals could go extinct.

> "You are to bring into the ark two of all living creatures, male and female, to keep them alive with you."
>
> —God speaking to Noah, Genesis 6:19–6:20

AGAINST EXTINCTION

Inerrant: *adj.*, incapable of being wrong

In the seventeenth century, Europeans believed that the Bible was inerrant. Every word of it was true. So when God ordered Noah to save all the living creatures on Earth, all the living creatures were saved. Nothing went extinct.

Christians at the time believed in the theory of a "great chain of being." That is, all life on Earth was an unbroken line that started from the lowest worm and led all the way up to humans, and then angels and God. To break that chain meant breaking the order of God's plan. John Ray, the best-known naturalist at the time, said that the loss of even a single species of animal would be like a "dismembering of the universe."

God, said Ray, was "especially concerned to preserve and secure all the works of creation." Since God created the universe perfectly, any creature going extinct would make the universe imperfect. Anyone arguing for the idea of extinction was literally arguing against the perfection of God.

Hooke was not an especially religious man, but he knew better than to argue with religion. In public, he said that perhaps there *were* living ammonites somewhere out in the world . . . they simply hadn't been discovered yet. In the seventeenth century, explorers were still traveling the globe, discovering new lands and new species all the time. In private, however, Hooke speculated that it was possible for animals to go extinct.

Perhaps, Hooke thought, the past looked very different from the present. This was a radical idea. To the biblical literalists at the time, Earth had always existed exactly as God had made it. In 1668, Hooke got up in front of the members of the Royal Society and gave a lecture that marked an important change in the way humans thought about fossils. He said:

"How trivial a thing a rotten shell may appear to some, yet these monuments of nature are more certain tokens of [the past] than coins or medals. . . ."

At that time, archeology was a brand-new concept. Historians were collecting ancient scrolls, pottery, weapons, and coins, and using them to understand the workings of the long-lost Roman and Greek Empires. Hooke proposed that scientists treat fossils the way historians treat antique coins and books. Except instead of using them to understand ancient empires, fossils could be used to understand Earth's past.

Even a man of Hooke's massive ego seemed to understand that he was not quite up to the full challenge. Human knowledge simply wasn't advanced far enough. With a touch of humility, he confessed, "It is very difficult to read them. . . .

"Yet," he said, "it is not impossible."

Hooke's idea slowly caught on. Over the next two centuries, fossil hunters started referring to fossils as "nature's coins." Fossils were no longer mysterious works of mythology, crystals, or plastic.

Fossils were clues to the past.

That meant scientists were now detectives. To understand fossils, their next task was to gather as many clues as they could find.

"The game is afoot."
—SHERLOCK HOLMES

PART 3

THE COLLECTORS

DEATH IN THE ARK

A detective and a scientist perform the same job. They both want to solve a mystery. To do that, they gather as much information as possible. The only difference is that a detective calls the information clues and a scientist calls it data. Once they assemble that information together, they can see patterns form. They can begin to solve the case.

Dr. Plot's single fossil bone wasn't enough to solve the mystery of dinosaurs' existence. A few fossilized seashells or shark teeth wouldn't decode the past. But if you assemble enough fossils together, you can start to form what paleontologists refer to as "a fossil record." Then the patterns form and you can begin to shed light onto the past.

To create a fossil record, you need to collect fossils. For the longest time, most people didn't think this was something worth doing. When fossils were simply "formed stones," they weren't given any particular value. In the seventeenth century, that began to change.

This is the story of the fossil record that led to the discovery of *Megalosaurus*.

It eventually grew to become one of the largest fossil records in the world at the time, but it began very humbly in a gardener's house in London, at 274 South Lambeth Road.

This was not a normal home. It was the family home of John Tradescant the Younger; his wife, Hester; and their two young children, but it was also considered one of the wonders of the world. The house even had its own name—the Ark, or sometimes, Tradescant's Ark.

The Tradescant home, aka Tradescant's
Ark, South Lambeth Road, London.

The British called a collection like this a cabinet of curiosities, but the Germans had an even better name for it—a *wunderkammer*, or "wonder room." Tradescant's Ark was so wondrous that when it opened to the public (for a small fee), it became one of the largest tourist attractions in London. Perhaps that is why, if you walked into the backyard of the large stone house on Lambeth Road on April 4, 1678, you would have seen the greatest curiosity of all. . . .

Hester Tradescant, the widow of John Tradescant and rightful heir to the Ark, lying facedown in her shallow fishpond.

She was dead.

Drowned.

The authorities never solved the case, but whispers around London told a different tale. . . . She had been murdered. And everyone knew the reason why.

Like Noah's Ark from the Bible, it was said that Tradescant's Ark contained every animal on Earth. The only difference was that Tradescant's animals were stuffed and mounted. The entrance to the Ark was a tunnel made from the rib bones of a whale.

The collection wasn't just stuffed animals. The house was filled from floor to ceiling with every plant, flower, and seed known at the time. There were exotic man-made items from the far reaches of the British Empire—a Native American headdress, Egyptian trinkets, masks from Borneo, silks and beads from India. But for scientific research, the most important part of the collection was its rocks, minerals, and fossils from all over the globe.

THE CURIOUS BEGINNING

The idea of a cabinet of curiosities didn't start with Tradescant. It began about a hundred years earlier with exactly the sort of people you would expect to have large collections of stuff—kings, dukes, barons, the royalty of Europe.

Every royal palace had the usual paintings and statues lying around. But during the Age of Exploration in the fourteenth and fifteenth centuries, European rulers began to add objects from foreign countries to their collections as well. Explorers like Christopher Columbus and Vasco da Gama landed in North America, South America, India, Asia, Africa, and in many cases, conquered the locals with violence. They sent samples of these foreign cultures (weapons, money, clothing) back home, where the king would collect them as "exotic" mementos of his empire.

At the same time, the Scientific Revolution was generating enthusiasm for the wonder of the natural world. Kings began to prize plants, animals, and minerals as well. They even added a few "rarities" from the natural world to wow their guests. There were fakes like a mermaid (in reality, a monkey with a fish tail sewed onto it) or a baby dragon (a rat with lizard parts glued on).

But among these rarities you could also find the first organized collections of dinosaur fossils, though nobody knew it. In the 1500s, the king of Hapsburg's collection contained the bones of a giant human and a dragon's egg (needless to say, both actually came from dinosaurs).

The idea of collecting began to trickle down from the great lords of Europe to more common folk. Or at least, the few common folk who were able to travel far and wide enough to collect "curiosities." One of the earliest people afforded this opportunity was the father of John Tradescant the Younger. His name was, naturally, John Tradescant the Elder.

During the 1500s, he was the head gardener for some of the most prominent aristocrats in England, including the

John Tradescant the Elder (1570s–1638).

Barbary Coast of Algiers. Like any tourist, Tradescant collected mementos of his adventures. Plants, animals, costumes, coins, whatever caught his eye. He created his own cabinet of curiosities.

As his collection swelled, he began to take it more seriously. Before his sailor friends set out to sea, he asked them to bring back "all manner of beasts & Fowl & birds." Beyond that, he simply wanted "any thing that is strange."

WONDER TO THE PEOPLE

When John the Elder died, his son, John the Younger, inherited many things from his father—his love for travel, his love of collecting, and he even inherited his father's job with the queen as "Keeper of Her Majesty's Gardens, Vines, and Silkworms."

Most importantly, he inherited his father's collection.

John the Younger devoted his free time to organizing and arranging it. Eventually, sometime around 1634, he did something that no one had ever done before . . . he opened the Ark to the public. Tradescant had just created the world's very first public museum.

Before Tradescant, seeing a wonder room was impossible without an invitation from royalty. Perhaps because the

queen herself. This was a position of great responsibility. The garden of an aristocrat was like the tail of a peacock. It was a display of their wealth and power. Tradescant the Elder's bosses sent him all over the world in search of exotic plants and trees that could enhance their gardens (and reputations).

The Elder's traveling seemed to give him a taste for adventure. At one point, he took a leave of absence from his gardening work so he could fight pirates along the

John Tradescant the Younger (1608–1662).

RITRATTO DEL MVSEO DI FERRANTE IMPERATO

꩜ THE MOST CURIOUS OF CURIOSITIES ꩜

Here are some of the more "curious" curiosities gathered in those early seventeenth-century cabinets.

- ☞ The skull of a narwhal

- ☞ An ape's head

- ☞ "Outlandish fruits"

- ☞ The skull of the collector's favorite composer

- ☞ An image of Jesus carved on a cherry pit

- ☞ A meteorite that fell from the sky and landed on a monk's head (he died)

- ☞ Two feathers of a phoenix's tail

- ☞ A Scythian lamb—a fuzzy fern thought to be a cross between a fern and a sheep

- ☞ A vial of blood that rained from the sky

- ☞ "A cheese" (There are no details about what made this a "curious" cheese.)

Tradescants were commoners themselves, they understood the value of showing the natural world to the public. What was even more unusual for the time was that Tradescant allowed both men *and* women to enter. For sixpence (about the price of a pound of butter), all visitors were welcome to not just view the collection but touch it as well.

One German visitor was appalled that "country folk" were allowed to "handle everything in the usual English fashion . . . they run here and there, grabbing at everything." Their excitement was understandable. For many English people, it was their first chance to get a glimpse of the world outside England—a Native American canoe, foreign shoes, the head of a tiger, and even the rare and seldom seen dodo bird. Not only that, it was their chance to see what was *underneath* England. There were "a number of things changed into stone," like a "human" bone that weighed 42 pounds.

The scientific value of these cabinets was questionable. Some sniffed that Tradescant's Ark should be renamed "the knick-knackery." Cabinets of curiosities were primar-

The most famous cabinet in Europe was built by a Dutchman named Frederik Ruysch. He filled a room with the skeletons of children in a variety of poses such as crying into handkerchiefs and playing the violin.

ily built to be entertaining. There are no images of what the Ark looked like on the inside, but it would have been very similar to some of the other cabinets around Europe at the time, like the one pictured on the previous page, which was collected by a Danish man with the fantastic name of Ole Worm.

Despite the Ark's popularity, Tradescant wanted to gain respect in the scientific community. To do that, he needed to publish a catalogue that listed all the pieces in his collection. This was a massive job, so he looked for help from someone well-versed in collecting specimens. He found a man named Elias Ashmole, who appeared to have the perfect background. Ashmole was a wealthy aristocrat, a member of the Royal Society, and a well-known collector in his own right.

What Tradescant didn't know was that Ashmole wasn't quite as noble as he seemed.

Elias Ashmole dressed for success.

collection. But in 1662, John the Younger died. That's when things took a darker turn.

After his death, Ashmole produced a document showing that John had willed the entire Ark over to him. John's widow, Hester, sued. She claimed that Ashmole had gotten her husband drunk one night and tricked him into signing the papers. After several years, the

ENTER ASHMOLE

Elias Ashmole was indeed quite wealthy. He came from a prominent family, but by the time he was born, they had lost their fortune. This sparked a burning desire in him to regain his status in society. When it came time to get married, Ashmole courted a number of rich widows and eventually married a woman who was 20 years older than him. After she died, he inherited her fortune and used it to become an avid student of astrology, alchemy, and botany.

At first, Ashmole's scientific credentials (and deep pockets) proved invaluable to Tradescant. Ashmole organized the collection and, in 1652, funded the publication of the entire catalogue himself. He even moved into the house next door to the Tradescants so he could be closer to the

The fairly glum widow, Hester Tradescant, and stepchildren, John and Frances, 1644.

courts sided with Ashmole. However, they noted, he could only take ownership of the collection once Hester died.

Ashmole began looking for a place that could house the collection once it came into his possession. After several years, he triumphantly announced that Oxford University agreed to house the collection. The learned Dr. Plot and his fellow fossil enthusiasts had developed an intense interest in the "formed stones" that were turning up with increased regularity in the quarries around Oxford. In fact, the university agreed to something completely new—it would construct a building for the sole purpose of being a museum. The Tradescant collection would be the centerpiece of this new museum's collection. There was just one problem with these plans.

Hester was still alive.

As a widow with two children, she had no source of income. Not only that, but she seemed to be having a nervous breakdown. Living literally next door to the man she blamed for stealing her husband's lifework seemed to drive her over the edge. Hester reported to the authorities that Elias cut a hole in the wall between their two houses and was stealing pieces of the Ark.

Outraged, Ashmole pressed charges against her, claiming that Hester's house had fallen into such disrepair that thieves had climbed up her compost heap, leaped over his wall, and stolen 32 of his chickens. Whether any of this was true or not

(authorities dismissed both charges), what was undeniable was that the collection was shrinking. In order to feed her family, Hester had begun selling off bits and pieces. The longer this went on, the less of the Ark would be left for Ashmole to inherit.

The original Ashmolean Museum, 1834.

Then on the evening of April 4, 1678, Ashmole noted coolly in his diary: "My wife told me that Mrs. Tradescant was found drowned in her pond. She was drowned the day before about noon . . . by some circumstance."

Two weeks later, Ashmole began removing paintings from the Tradescant house and placing them in his own home. For safekeeping, he assured officials.

Five years later, a brand-new museum (which still exists today) opened in Oxford, England, with his name permanently etched onto it—the Ashmolean Museum.

At the opening ceremony, Elias Ashmole explained that he gifted his collection to the university "because the knowledge of Nature is very necessary to human life and health."

Caring for such a large collection was a full-time occupation. Ashmole and the heads of Oxford agreed that the person best qualified for the job was the expert on all plant and animal life in the area—"the learned Dr. Plot." They appointed him to be the very first keeper of the Ashmolean, a building dedicated to the housing of curiosities and fossils.

Plot realized that this new museum was the perfect home for his own personal collection of curiosities, so he donated those as well. We don't know exactly what happened to the mysterious scrotum-y thighbone of the "giant." At some point, the actual fossil itself was lost (which demonstates just how little importance was placed on fossils at the time), but Plot's illustration survived.

Thus, a record of the first bone of *Megalosaurus* found its permanent home in an Oxford museum.

This was one of the most important steps in the discovery of dinosaurs. The simple idea of a building dedicated to collecting curiosities may sound trivial, but it was a place where all the local fossils could be brought together in one place. A fossil record could grow, patterns could form, and the first dinosaur could eventually come to light.

THE BONE MARKET

Creating a collection of curiosities was now a popular and respectable new hobby among the wealthy. The kings of Europe were doing it. Elias Ashmole did it and got a museum named after him! England's *Dictionary of National Biography* (sort of a Facebook for eighteenth-century aristocrats) noted that 177 noblemen and noblewomen were active fossil collectors.

However, certain adjustments had to be made. The early wonder rooms of the kings were exactly what their name implied—an entire room filled with knickknacks. Lesser aristocrats weren't quite wealthy enough to buy an entire roomful of curiosities (much less have an entire room to fill). That's when the name "cabinet of curiosities" became a bit more literal.

Gentlemen bought wooden cabinets so they could store and display their collections. Before TVs or radio, a gentleman was expected to offer some after-dinner amusement for his guests. This usually meant card games, musicians, or guest speakers, but the Scientific Revolution sparked people's interest in bones, pickled organs, and feathers (not to mention the occasional mermaid's hand).

In the natural world, nothing was more curious than fossils. Every good

A typical gentleman's cabinet of curiosities (1690s).

cabinet had to have at least a few, and the more exotic your fossils, the more you could impress your guests.

The cabinet of curiosities became a new form of entertainment.

This created a demand for fossils, and when wealthy people demand something, a marketplace will spring up to supply it. Fossils ceased to be a mere curiosity or something to be puzzled over by scientists. They were now a product that was worth money.

This was happening all over Europe. Instead of being tossed aside, fossils were now carefully collected and catalogued (by salesmen and scientists alike). By the mid-1700s, shops opened in London selling the fossilized bones of "whales." One of the busiest bone markets in Europe was in the town of Oxford.

Next to Old Slaughter's Coffee

House, a store began to sell fossils of "hippos," "elephants," and "crocodiles" that came from the local quarries. These labels were wrong, of course, but they point to the incredible variety of bones being dug up in the Oxford countryside. In fact, right outside town were some of the richest fossil sites in the country.

DIGGING FOR DINOSAURS

In 1096, Oxford University became the first university in England. This was significant because the physical act of building a school required building material.

In this case, stone. Since stone is so heavy to transport, the builders needed to get the materials from somewhere close to town.

Ten miles outside Oxford is a town known as Stonesfield. The name of the village comes from an Old English word meaning "fool's field," because only a fool would try to farm on that particular bit of land. The ground was far too rocky. So instead of

A Stonesfield miner in 1905 splitting ordinary limestone into valuable slate roofing tiles. Shaving into the past half an inch at a time like this, it's no wonder Stonesfield was such a hot spot for fossil discoveries.

Stonesfield village.

- STONESFIELD - 6

farming and selling food, the locals sold the rocks. The locals didn't know it, but those rocks contained the tomb of the megalosaurs that had died 160 million years ago.

Geologically, Britain is unique. It is one of the only places on Earth that contains every geological formation. No matter what sort of stone you are looking for, if you dig around long enough, you will find it. As the people of Stonesfield dug down, they discovered a particularly amazing type of rock. It had a lovely yellow color, but more importantly, it was soft enough to cut into easy-to-build-with blocks. It could even be split into wafer-thin layers that acted as roofing slate. The name of this rock was oolite limestone, and many of the original buildings of Oxford University were built with it.

The fame of Stonesfield oolite spread around the country. Wealthy homeowners were willing to pay top dollar so their roofs could look like the distinguished slate roofs of Oxford University. The possibility of making good money attracted laborers from all over the country. During one summer in the 1800s, a quarry a few miles away from Stonesfield that had a similar form of slate attracted an estimated *120,000* workers!

But the Stonesfield quarry itself was so small that only a handful of locals could work it at the same time. During this period, there were approximately 140 men who worked in the Stonesfield quarry, and out of those, only 20 worked full-time. It was those 20 who slowly, painstakingly chipped away at the exact layer of rock that contained the bones of *Megalosaurus*.

It was only a matter of time before they found . . .

THE SECOND BONE

It's no coincidence that the first dinosaur bone (Dr. Plot's) and the first dinosaur (*Megalosaurus*) came from Oxford.

In the quarries that dotted the Oxford countryside, the uneducated laborers didn't know anything about the Scientific Revolution. What they did know was that as they carved into the hills in search of slate, whenever they got about 60 feet underground they would start seeing fossilized plants, shells, teeth, and bones appear.

This was true of quarries all over Europe, but in Oxford the fascination with fossils was not some hot new trend. It had a deep tradition. Oxford was a place of higher learning. Long before aristocrats began buying fossils to pretty up their collections, the school's professors wanted good specimens to aid their understanding of the natural world. Not only that, but many of these scholars came from the upper classes of England. They had money to spend.

Whenever a laborer in the Stonesfield

quarries found a good fossil, he would put the fossil on display in the window of his home. In 1699, the second keeper of the Ashmolean, Edward Llwyd (Dr. Plot retired), went for a fossil-hunting walk through Stonesfield. In one of the worker's windows, he saw a curiosity that was *so* curious, he just had to buy it.

It was a tooth.

This tooth, however, very clearly did *not* belong to an elephant. It was sharp, the kind used to tear flesh. Perhaps, thought Llwyd, it belonged to some sort of large, unknown fish. It was actually the tooth of a *Megalosaurus*, but at the time, "fish" was a pretty reasonable guess.

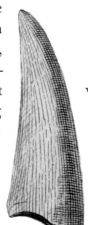

Illustration of a *Megalosaurus* tooth by Edward Llwyd, 1699. The actual fossil is now lost.

were seashells under the dry, desert sand of Egypt.

These fossilized sea creatures weren't just found underground. They were on top of mountains as well. The Rocky Mountains of North America are full of seashells. One seventeenth-century explorer traveled to South America in search of gold. After weeks of hiking up the Andes Mountains, he finally reached the peak, where he dug into the ground and found . . . seashells. *He was 13,000 feet above sea level!*

> ## "[The] origin of shells in high places [is] beyond the investigation of human [wisdom]."
>
> —THOMAS JEFFERSON

Fossilized turtle shells were also found in the Stonesfield quarry. In fact, fish skeletons and fossilized seashells were being found lodged in rocks all over the world. Priests in France noticed seashells inside the stone blocks used to make their cathedrals. The pope puzzled over seashells buried in the hills of Vatican City. There

This, of course, brings to mind a very simple, but very important, question:

How the heck did sea creatures get on top of a mountain?

Around the world, scientists and philosophers knew this as the Seashell Problem. Until it was solved, the discovery of dinosaurs (and the origins of all fossils)

could go no further. It drove some of the smartest people of the time to despair.

When Llwyd purchased the tooth from the Stonesfield quarries, he had no real answer to this question. So the tooth became just another curiosity, an unsolvable mystery. Llwyd brought it back to the Ashmolean Museum, where he stored it with the other fossils, including the illustration of the thighbone discovered by Dr. Plot.

The pieces of *Megalosaurus* were beginning to come together.

PART 4

THE WORLD MAKERS

IT BEGINS WITH A QUESTION

One of the most basic ways to understand a subject is to ask: "Who?" "What?" "When?" "Where?" "Why?" and "How?"

If humans used these questions to understand fossils (which would lead us to the discovery of dinosaurs), then it would look like this:

Because of Steno, we know *what* fossils are—the remains of animals.

Because of Hooke, we know *how* fossils are made—bones and plants are covered in water, mud, sand, etc., and absorb minerals until they become fossilized.

The next questions take us one step further into the past: *Where* do fossils come from? *Why* are they found in places that don't make sense?

These are the questions that form the Seashell Problem. There are no fish swimming on top of mountains, so how did their fossilized bones get up there? Elephants do not live underground, so why are their bones down there?

We didn't know it yet, but in order to answer the questions "where" and "why," we first needed to answer the question "when?"

Time, it turns out, is one of the most important pieces of the puzzle in understanding the origins of fossils.

Fossils come from things that lived and died over an immense period of time. Fossils are formed over immense periods of time. The earth around them moves and shifts over immense periods of time. None of this process works without time.

But we didn't understand that yet, because even as late as the eighteenth century, scientists had no idea that Earth even had a past.

"IN THE BEGINNING . . ."

The study of fossils is known as paleontology. It is defined as "the science of understanding life from Earth's past." It's actually a hybrid science—the combination of anatomy (the study of life) and geology (the study of Earth's past). By Steno's time, humans were beginning to understand anatomy. But before we could understand fossils, we needed to invent the science of geology.

In Europe, for over a thousand years, all geological thinking—our ideas about the origins and history of Earth—was contained in these four sentences:

"In the beginning, God created the Heaven and the Earth. . . . And God said, 'Let the waters under the heavens be gathered together into one place, and let dry land appear.' And it was so. God called the dry land 'Earth. . . .'"

—Genesis 1:1, 1:9–10

To biblical scholars, humans were the center of the Bible's story. God created Earth merely as a place for us to live. However, that changed in the seventeenth century when the Scientific Revolution inspired scientists to measure things—the force of gravity, the movements of the stars, and with the building of mechanical clocks, even the movement of time itself. Some scholars became fascinated with the Bible's opening phrase: "In the beginning . . ."

All science begins with a question—from a child's first experiment at a school science fair to entire fields of study.

"What are the lights in the night sky?" became astronomy.

"How does the human body work?" become anatomy.

Geology began with this: "*When was the beginning?*" "Exactly how old is Earth?"

To explain the existence of fossils, every culture created stories—myths—about giants, monsters, and dragons. In much the same way, every culture has a myth that explains the creation of Earth.

Chinese mythology tells the story of a giant that lived inside an egg for 18,000 years until the egg broke apart. The giant grew for another 18,000 years, and when he finally died, his body became the land and his blood became the rivers. Australian aborigines have the oldest continuous culture in history, dating back almost 60,000 years. In their mythology, there was a time before humans that stretched back into eternity.

In seventeenth-century Europe, global exploration was slow and incomplete. European scholars (who were Christian) either hadn't yet encountered these older cultures, didn't understand them, or simply ignored them. Since the science of geology began in Western Europe, it began with European scholars trying to understand their own creation myth—Genesis, the first chapter in the Holy Bible.

No one was more qualified to do this than James Ussher. As the archbishop of the Church of Ireland, Ussher was a powerful religious authority in the seventeenth century. More importantly, he was reputed to own the world's largest personal library. Before computers, books were the only way that knowledge and data could be stored and passed down through the generations. With his library, Ussher had more historical knowledge within arm's reach than almost any other person in Europe.

Inspired by the Scientific Revolution, Ussher began to measure how much *time* was in the

James Ussher, the first geologist and the best-read man in Europe (1581–1656).

Bible, all the way back to "the beginning." Ussher was no lone genius. Many scholars (including Sir Isaac Newton) were attempting the same calculations, but Ussher was the most meticulous. He measured birth records and books of ancient Roman and Greek history. He used lunar calendars, leap years, and astronomical records of eclipses and comets as well. The gargantuan effort took him ten years and almost 2,000 pages to complete. Finally, in 1650, he came to a conclusion:

Earth was formed on Sunday, October 23, 4004 B.C. . . . . around lunchtime.

4004 B.C.

Modern science tells us that this number is wrong by approximately 4,499,994,000 years. But historians regard Ussher's date as the first time that someone tried to calculate the age of Earth. This was the birth of geology.

In 1703, the Church of England printed an updated version of the King James Bible, the most popular version of the Bible in the world, and included Ussher's dates in the margins. From that point on, Christians thought Ussher's numbers were as much a part of the Bible as the words themselves.

The year 4004 B.C. became part of the

• • • • • • • • • • • • • • • •

A Powerful Idea

Ussher's estimated date is one of the most influential ideas in human history. It was only in 1978 that Ussher's dates were removed from the Gideons Bibles that are placed in every hotel room in America. Perhaps that helps explain why approximately 40 percent of Americans still believe that Earth was created 6,000 years ago.

• • • • • • • • • • • • • • • •

religious education of every man, woman, and child in England.

THE BIRTH OF A GEOLOGIST

Every child in eighteenth-century England read the Bible. It was part of their daily prayers, education, and entertainment. But William Buckland read it more than most. He was the son of a reverend. Multiple times every day, he would open his Bible and see the words "In the beginning . . ." and next to it the date: "4004 B.C."

The idea that Earth was 6,000 years old was ingrained in his mind.

But the Bible wasn't William's only education. He was born in 1784 in the south of England in the small market town of Axminster. The town was surrounded by forests, and William spent a great deal of time in nature. He developed a particular talent for climbing trees and stealing eggs from birds' nests.

His father, the Reverend Charles Buckland, encouraged William's love of the outdoors. He frequently took William along with him on his daily walks to the local rock quarries. One of a reverend's duties was to help oversee the upkeep of the town. Reverend Buckland was in charge of the local roads. The constant rain in England turned any dirt road into impassable mud. To prevent this, towns spread their roads with gravel, which they mined from local quarries.

Axminster is just five miles from the

The River Axe in William Buckland's hometown of Axminster. Buckland grew up very close to this exact spot.

seaside town of Lyme Regis. The cliffs of Lyme Regis are so full of fossils that it was later named "the Jurassic Coast." Within a few decades, it would become one of the most important sites in the history of fossil hunting. This made the Axminster quarries an excellent spot for fossil hunting too.

William's father became such an avid collector of fossils that he was part of a group in England known as the Divines. "The Divines" was the nickname given to a whole generation of small-town reverends who became fascinated with fossil hunting. By the eighteenth century, the curiosity collections of the aristocrats had become so fashionable (and respectable) that the habit trickled down to the clergy. In the sleepy country villages of England,

the reverend was usually the most educated person in town, and fossil collecting was a form of intellectual stimulation. They believed that if God created Earth, then He created fossils as well. By investigating and understanding fossils, they could better understand God.

Charles Buckland shared his love of fossil hunting with William. On weekends, they would occasionally travel five miles south to the beaches of Lyme Regis. There, the seaside cliffs are laid out in a pattern that looks distinctly like the pages of a great book. William and his father spent many pleasant afternoons together, walking along the beach and scanning the

The cliffs of Lyme Regis. The Jurassic Coast, England.

pages of that cliff for fossils they could marvel over. Young William formed a powerful connection between his love of Earth and God.

While he spent his free time pondering fossils with his father, William did not neglect his studies. In fact, he proved to be a remarkably bright student. Despite his humble background, William Buckland was accepted into the prestigious Oxford University.

So in 1801, at the age of 17, William said good-bye to his mother and father and boarded a carriage bound for Oxford. He was headed toward a remarkable life as one of England's most famous scientists.

Despite being raised on Ussher's ideas, William would become Oxford's very first professor of geology, responsible for exploring much further into Earth's past than 6,000 years. He would discover creatures that no one at the time could imagine.

> William Buckland would grow up to be the man who'd announce the discovery of the first dinosaur— *Megalosaurus.*

But as the carriage slowly carried him away from his childhood home, William must have noticed that the road that eased his path to a bright future was covered with gravel and bits of ground-up fossil. It was a road he and his father had built together.

THE EDUCATION OF A CREATIONIST

The Bible does not mention dinosaurs or even slightly oversized reptiles. The King James Bible stated that Earth was 6,000 years old. So how could a boy raised on that belief become a man who believed in dinosaurs that existed millions of years ago?

William Buckland took the first steps on that journey when he arrived at Oxford University. At that time, an Oxford education was primarily religious and historical. The university was actually the theological center for the Church of England. Almost every professor was an ordained minister. At first, that suited Buckland just fine. He was studying to become a reverend like his father.

As an institution, Oxford was largely indifferent to the sciences at that time, but exciting things were beginning to happen. The quarries outside Oxford were yielding a steady stream of fossils. Combined with the Ashmolean/Tradescant collection, the university's fossil collection was one of the best in the world. They began to offer a handful of science classes, which Buckland attended with interest. He had, after all, been raised by a fossil-hunting "Divine."

There was a class on anatomy, where Buckland would learn about Nicolaus Steno's discoveries linking fossils and shark teeth. There was also a class on mineralogy (the word "geology" was barely known at that point). One of the first rules Buckland would learn in that class is something that is taught to beginning geology students even today. It is known as Steno's law of superposition. The same Nicolaus Steno who transformed the study of anatomy is also known as the Father of Geology. He was a busy guy.

Oxford University. Note the yellowish color of the buildings—that's the color of the oolite limestone.

After Steno published his study of the shark's head in 1667, he couldn't stop thinking about the fossilized shark teeth known as tongue-stones. He became so obsessed with their origin that he abandoned his anatomical studies, packed his bags, and traveled to their source—the island of Malta.

THE FIRST LAW

Steno didn't write much about the details of his Malta trip. We know he visited the mountains and cliffs to examine where tongue-stones were found. He visited several mines, and examined the rocks underground. This sounds like an obvious thing to do, but the idea of examining actual dirt and rocks was a completely new idea.

Until that point, when people like Ussher wanted to learn about Earth, they studied the Bible. But Steno had a geolog-

and when it rained, the essence seeped into the rocks and fish grew there. Steno rejected the idea of raining shark babies, not because it was too good to be true, but because the evidence didn't support it.

He reasoned that if something grows inside a solid object, like a baby chick inside an egg, it will eventually grow large enough to crack that object. But there was no sign of the rocks around the tongue-stones

> **"All truths are easy to understand once they are discovered. The point is to discover them."**
>
> —GALILEO

ical question that the Bible didn't answer: How does a solid object like a shark tooth or a seashell get *inside* another solid object like a rock? How does a shark tooth get inside a cliff high above the water?

He was trying to solve the Seashell Problem.

By then, many people had come up with answers, but they tended to be . . . imaginative. Some believed that the "essence" of fish rose up from the ocean in vapors,

being cracked. The only way Steno could explain "a solid inside a solid" was if the inner object (the tooth or shell) came first, and then the rock formed around it. But this led to an even larger question:

How do rocks form? *How* was Earth made?

Again, Steno struggled with ancient myths. The Bible said that Earth was simply willed into existence by God overnight. But this didn't explain how things formed afterward. Farmers in Malta believed that stones were male or female, they had sex, and gave birth to baby stones. Steno rejected this and reached for a more logical answer.

If you find a seashell on dry ground, then at some point in the past, that piece of ground must have been covered by the sea. A shell lying on the ocean floor will slowly be covered in a layer of sand and sediment. Through time and pressure, that soft sediment layer will condense and harden into a layer of rock.

That is how a solid can be inside another solid—if it forms in a layer. This type of rock is now called "sedimentary."

As he stared at the cliffs of Malta, Steno's training as an anatomist must have kicked in. He had spent his whole life learning to slice through and identify layers of the human body—skin, fat, tissue, muscle, and bone. So when he looked at the cliffs, he noticed that, "In various places, I have seen that Earth is composed of layers superimposed on each other."

He sketched a simple diagram to show how he thought the cliffs were formed. Visually, it's not the most exciting piece of art, but it's one of the most important images in the history of science.

This became Steno's first law of superposition, and it's quite simple—rocks form in flat layers on top of each other. Even hills, mountains, and cliffs full of tongue-stones start as flat layers and are pushed up and broken by other forces (earthquakes, erosion, etc.) so they begin to look like this:

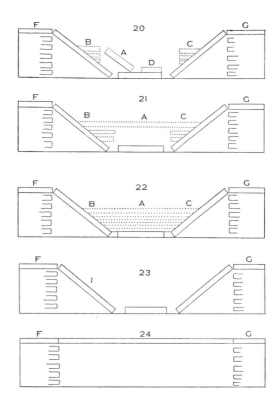

Above: When there is a disturbance in the ground (earthquake, landslide, etc.), the layers collapse in regular patterns, but can still be found underneath.

Left: Steno's illustration of how sediment/ rock forms in layers, 1669.

Try it for yourself. Next time you're near a hill where you can see the exposed rock layers, you'll see that those layers are at an angle. Steno's law is simple, but what it *means* is incredibly profound— since each layer takes time to form, the bottom layers are the oldest and every layer above it gets increasingly younger as it goes up. In other words, *layers of rock are a timeline of Earth's history.*

Back in England, some of William Buckland's fellow students didn't get it. Percy Bysshe Shelley, one of the most famous Romantic poets in England, attended a mineralogy class at Oxford and walked out halfway through, saying, "It was so stupid. . . . Stones, stones, stones! Nothing but stones!"

But Buckland, with his childhood memories of the layered cliffs of Lyme Regis, understood it well.

> Geology is not the study of stones. It is the study of time. Rocks are the ticking clocks that measure the age of Earth.

As for the young, upper layers of rock that contained shark teeth and sea-shells, how could water rise high enough to create these layers on top of moun-tains? Like Ussher and Buckland, Steno was highly religious and he believed that "the book of nature and the books of the Bible were complementary." So when it came to water on mountaintops and bur-ied animals, Steno was excited because he believed that the Bible had a very clear answer.

It wasn't just Steno. Every scholar at the time believed that the answer to the Seashell Problem (and thus, the source of all fossils) was the Bible's story of Noah's Ark and the great flood that covered the world. It took centuries for scholars to move past this theory and discover the far older age of Earth. Ironically, the idea that gave them this breakthrough was Steno's first law.

THE GREAT FLOOD

Beside the creation story in Genesis, there is only one other world-shaping, geological event in the Bible—Noah's flood, also known as the deluge.

Almost every culture in the world has a flood story in its mythology. In fact, flood stories are so common that many anthropologists believe there *was* some sort of flooding event that took place in early human history (possibly related to the melting of the Ice Age glaciers). But much like Ussher, the only source of infor-mation that European scholars had about the past was the Bible. Anyone looking for clues about fossils analyzed and argued

over the Bible's flood story, which goes like this:

> **W**hen the Lord created humans, they quickly spread across Earth. But they soon became wicked, so the Lord decided to destroy them. However, one man named Noah was virtuous, so the Lord decided to spare his life. He told Noah to build a massive boat, an ark, and bring on board his family and seven pairs of every kind of animal.
>
> Then it rained for forty days and forty nights. The ark floated safely on the waters as they rose and increased greatly on Earth. All the high mountains under the entire heavens were covered and "the waters flooded the earth for a hundred and fifty days."
>
> —Genesis 7

For centuries, this story was used to explain any fossil in any location—it was simply an animal killed and buried by the flood. But Steno wasn't the only person to become fascinated with our planet's past. A group of religious scholars and philosophers latched on to Steno's idea of explaining Earth through observation. They stopped relying on the Bible's explanation of how Earth formed and started using logic and reason.

This was the next step in the formation of geology, and the group became known as the World Makers.

THE WORLD MAKERS

The World Makers were storytellers.

They had no experiments or data to back up their theories (science was still in its infancy then), but they wanted their stories to make sense. As you will soon see, none of their ideas were even remotely accurate (most are downright laughable), but they still managed to accomplish something important. They *disproved* the theories taken from the Bible.

This wasn't their intention. The World Makers were, for the most part, men of God (reverends and priests), but as they examined the physical world and worked through their ideas, they received an unexpected surprise. They realized that there were problems with the Bible's version of Earth's creation. Mainly, there simply wasn't enough time. Ussher's dates were wrong, and fossils had nothing to do with the great flood.

When blind men touch different parts

of an elephant, they imagine a rope, a spear, or a wall. None of them have the correct answer. However, if you put their answers together, you can see a shape appear. When the World Makers imagined Earth, the shapes they saw were an egg, pudding, and fire.

1⟩ An Egg

Thomas Burnet was the personal priest to King William III of England. Together, they made a royal visit to Switzerland,

where the Swiss mountains were so awe inspiring, so different from the gentle hills of England, that Burnet began to wonder how Earth could form such dissimilar shapes.

Burnet proposed that God originally made Earth like an egg—perfectly smooth on the outside, with water underneath. When the "egg" cracked, mountains formed and the water came rushing out. To Burnet, Earth as we know it is "a dirty little planet . . . a world lying in its rubbish."

The cover of his book, *The Sacred Theory of the Earth*, actually illustrates his theory.

We could write this off as nonsense, but Burnet did something else that was very useful. He calculated all the water on Earth and decided that even with an additional forty days and nights of rain, there would not be enough water to cover the mountaintops during the flood. Therefore, he argued that the Bible *could not be taken literally*. There must be another, more rational explanation.

Another problem with the biblical flood story is that Earth was only covered with water for 150 days. However, Steno showed that the ground is made of

On the left is Burnet's "smooth egg" Earth. Moving counterclockwise, we see the "eggshell" collapse, the continents form, the floods cover most land, and finally . . . death. 1681.

"The leading idea which is present in all our research, and which accompanies every fresh observation . . . Time! Time! Time!"

—GEORGE SCROPE,
ENGLISH GEOLOGIST

multiple layers, some of them hundreds of feet thick, formed one by one over time. It was simply not possible for these layers to be created in 150 days.

2⟩ Pudding

Dr. John Woodward, a member of the Royal Society, disagreed. Perhaps, he said, when the flood came, gravity *stopped* and everything floated up into the air in a soup. (Remember, gravity had only been dreamed up a few years earlier by Sir Isaac Newton, so their understanding of it was still a bit sketchy.) When gravity restarted, everything congealed back together, with the heavier things (like fossils) on the bottom and lighter things (like dirt) on top. Some critics called this Woodward's "pudding" theory of Earth. Others were less kind: "The Doctor should have calculated the Proportions of his Drugs before he mixed them."

Those were fighting words. At a meeting of the Royal Society to discuss fossil shells, Woodward and one of his critics "became so heated that [one member] drew his sword." Several gentlemen had to step in to prevent "Philosophical blood [being] spilt."

3⟩ Fire

In France, an aristocrat named Count de Buffon believed that the planets were actually chunks of molten metal that a passing comet tore off the sun. These chunks then slowly cooled enough to form solid land.

To test this idea, he used a blacksmith's forge to heat metal balls and measured how long it took for them to cool down. He then estimated that Earth must be around 70,000 years old. In private, though, he told his friends that he thought the number was closer to 1 million. The fact that God played no part in Buffon's theory proved too much for the religious authorities of France. They forced him to print an apology.

Despite this, the World Makers opened the floodgates for new nonbiblical theories of Earth's creation. And every new theory pushed Earth's age further back into the past.

THE BUCKLANDS ON THE BEACH

Flood! Fire! Antigravity! Sword fights at the Royal Society!

The few students at Oxford who were interested in science were getting a darn good show. In the early 1800s, geology was the equivalent of quantum physics or artificial intelligence today. It was the cutting edge of science, with new discoveries being made all the time.

In his first year at Oxford, William Buckland was still just a teenager and he was enthralled. He was studying full-time to be a minister, but he attended every science class that Oxford offered, just for pleasure. Despite this heavy workload, he traveled back to Axminster as often as possible to take care of his family. During his first year away at school, his father, Charles, was in a terrible accident that left him blind.

William insisted on keeping their father-son tradition alive. He took his blind father to Lyme Regis so they could walk along the same beaches they had visited when he was a child. Only this time, William would lead, gently guiding his father by the arm.

When they found a new fossil in the sea cliff, William would lovingly describe it so his father could picture every detail. He would tell his father about all the exciting, new scientific ideas he'd been exposed to at Oxford. His father could no longer see, but William's eyes were open to a whole new world.

William would tell his father that geology had moved on from the World Makers. Some members of the Royal Society had become so fascinated with Earth that in 1807, they formed their own group—the Geological Society.

The Geological Society quickly separated into warring factions with competing theories, but what both groups agreed on was that all of this took time. Their Earth was far older than Ussher's. Their reasoning was simple—the Bible may say that the world was 6,000 years old, but "for the Almighty a thousand years is as one day."

Eventually, they all unified around the ideas of James Hutton.

James Hutton grew up on a farm in Scotland, but like Steno, he studied to become an anatomist. Doctors at the time were just beginning to understand the human circulation system—how the bloodstream constantly flushes away waste and regenerates itself. When Hutton returned to his farm in Scotland, he looked at the rocks in the ground, and the nearby mountains and sea, and saw the same sort of circulation system at work.

Earthquakes and volcanoes push mountains up out of the ground. Rivers and oceans erode the land and mountains away. This is Earth's circulation system—a constant process of destruction and regeneration that has been going on since the beginning of time.

Hutton's ideas are usually summed up

James Hutton, the father of modern geology, 1776. Also a physician, chemist, naturalist, and farmer.

by the phrase "The present is the key to the past." In other words, whatever geological action that we see, no matter how small, can explain any geological formation if you give it enough time. A waterfall pouring off a cliff has been falling on the rocks below for a long, long time, cracking them apart, washing them away, tearing down the mountain one pebble at a time.

But for how long? Hutton's answer was shocking and exciting. At a minimum, he believed Earth was millions of years old. Truthfully, he thought it was eternal. He saw "no vestige of a beginning, no prospect of an end."

Hutton wrote all of this in a book that was so dense, so difficult to understand (and so badly written), that no ordinary person read it. But geologists did, and that book became the basis of all modern geology.

William Buckland would then have told

his father about the life-changing decision he'd made. He attended Oxford to become a reverend, but ever since he was a child, the cliffs of Lyme Regis "were my geological school. They stared me in the face. They wooed me and caressed me, saying at every turn, 'Pray, pray be a geologist!'"

Buckland was answering those prayers. Now that the history of Earth was older than 6,000 years, the past was vast and completely unknown. If you had a taste for adventure, for discovering alien worlds (and alien creatures) that no human had ever seen, then geology was for you.

William Buckland decided to become a geologist.

A 19th-century depiction of geological forces—volcano, earthquake, precipitation, waterfall, flood, erosion.

> "Geologists . . .
> are engaged in
> reawakening the memory
> of the world."
>
> —A LAND,
> BY JACQUETTA HAWKES

THE THIRD BONE

There was something else that drew William Buckland to a life of geology. The science students at Oxford were witnessing a steady stream of fossils flow into the Ashmolean from the nearby quarries. Among the ammonites and fish bones, they could see that there were larger, more mysterious creatures lurking underground.

DIAGRAM OF
NATURAL PHENOMENA.
SHOWING THE PRINCIPAL CAUSES OF GEOLOGICAL CHANGES ON THE EARTH'S SURFACE.

In 1797, Buckland's anatomy professor, Sir Christopher Pegge, purchased the remarkable jawbone pictured below. This was a particularly important discovery for a number of reasons.

It came from the Stonesfield quarry, of course, just like the "fish tooth" discovered by the Ashmolean's second keeper. If they had placed the two side by side, they could have seen the similarities between the teeth, but they couldn't do that . . . *because the museum had lost the "fish tooth" and Dr. Plot's thighbone!*

A collection is only as good as the people who care for it, and in the 100 years between Dr. Plot, the second keeper, and Sir Pegge, many of the museum keepers simply didn't care about the fossils in the collection. Some fossils were lost, some were stolen, and some simply crumbled into dust.

In the 121 years that passed between the discovery of Dr. Plot's thighbone and this jawbone, a lot had changed. Fossils had gained prize-worthy status. This particular piece was truly spectacular. It wasn't a piece of bone or a single tooth. It was an entire section of a jaw. So Sir Pegge made sure that it was well preserved and cared for.

This jawbone became the first *Megalosaurus* fossil that has actually survived into the modern day. As the fossil record grew, our understanding of the past began to accelerate. After the discovery of this third bone, it would only take another 27 years to fit together the pieces to form the first dinosaur.

But until then, everyone was still guessing about what it represented. As one of Pegge's star students, Buckland would have certainly been allowed to marvel over it with his professor. They all agreed that it must have been some sort of crocodile.

But how did a "crocodile" get lodged in the rocks of a quarry that was 70 miles from the nearest ocean? Despite knowing that the timelines of the Bible were wrong, their best guess was still Noah's flood. This wasn't due to deep religious beliefs; they simply had no other ideas to work with. The science of geology hadn't made enough progress yet to give them other options to choose from.

A modern photograph of the actual *Megalosaurus* jawbone discovered in Stonesfield. Currently on display in the Oxford University Museum of Natural History.

Besides natural philosophers like the World Makers and the hobbyists of the Geological Society, no one cared enough about the physical makeup of the planet to study it. That was all about to change.

In fact, all of human civilization was changing, and the thing that changed it was coal.

. . . .

Deep Time

In 1956, scientists finally calculated the true age of Earth—4.5 *billion* years old.

Compared to the length of a human life, this number is so immense that it's hard for us to comprehend how incredibly *old* that really is. A geologist/writer named John McPhee described this by coining the phrase "deep time." Instead of numbers, he believes we should think of it in images.

Imagine that the age of Earth is the distance from the tip of your nose to the tip of your outstretched hand. If you stroke a nail file across the nail of your middle finger, you will have erased human history.

Another geologist, Keith Heyer Meldahl, explained how deep time affects Earth itself:

"[Erosion can] seem trivially slow in human time [but] can accomplish stunning work in geologic time. Let the Colorado River erode its bed by 1/100th of an inch each year (about the thickness of one of your fingernails). Multiply it by six million years, and you've carved the Grand Canyon."

Early geologists in Western Europe struggled with this concept, but older cultures had a better sense of Earth's true timescales. Korean mythology has a unit of time that is measured like this: Imagine a granite mountain that is 1 mile high. Every 1,000 years, an angel flies down from heaven and brushes the mountain's peak with her wings. When this happens so many times that the mountain is worn down to sea level . . . that is one unit of time.

PART 5

THE MAP OF TIME

GLOWING EMBER

It's fitting that the next great step in understanding dinosaurs came from the study of their remains. Except it wasn't fossilized bones, it was fossil fuel.

> "Let me tell you next of stones that burn like logs."
>
> —MARCO POLO, IN THIRTEENTH-CENTURY CHINA

Very early in human civilization, we discovered that when a certain type of black rock was heated, it would burn longer and hotter than regular wood. The Germans referred to it as *kohle*, their word for "glowing ember." English speakers turned that word into "coal."

The Chinese used it for heating over 3,000 years ago. In Europe, the Greeks used it to fire their metal forges as early as 400 B.C. In the second century A.D., when the Romans rode their war elephants into Britain, they discovered that coal was so plentiful it was literally lying on the ground.

The island of Britain sits on top of vast seams of the stuff. Romans began shipping it around the country, using it for everything from weapon making to heating their public bathhouses. However, even in those early days, people recognized that coal was an incredibly dirty fuel. By the thirteenth century, the city of London banned its use after it created toxic smog clouds over the city. In response, people searched for (relatively) cleaner forms of coal, and they eventually found it. Underground.

In 1575, the first coal mine in Britain opened up, but water kept flooding the mines, making it impossible to dig too deep. The solution came in 1698, when an Englishman named Thomas Savery invented the steam engine. It was cumbersome and used enormous amounts of fuel, but the miners had plenty of coal to feed it, so they used it to pump the water out of the mines.

It's incredible to think that such a simple machine (it had *no* moving parts) could have such an enormous impact on civilization, but over the next few decades, improvements made the steam engine more efficient and more powerful. This allowed miners to dig more coal, which encouraged mine owners to build more steam engines to do more types of jobs. By the late 1700s, steam engines powered mills, breweries, and a brand-new invention, the factory.

This was the birth of the Industrial Revolution. Like the Scientific Revolution, it was one of the greatest transformations in human history. To work in the factories, people left their farms. City populations exploded. Steam trains connected cities to each other. And all of it was powered by coal.

Before this time, the study of geology was reserved for eccentrics, curiosity collectors, and aristocratic oddballs like the World Makers. Once the steam engine was invented, however, governments and businesses suddenly became interested in learning more about the ground beneath their feet.

That's when geology got serious. That's when engineers got involved.

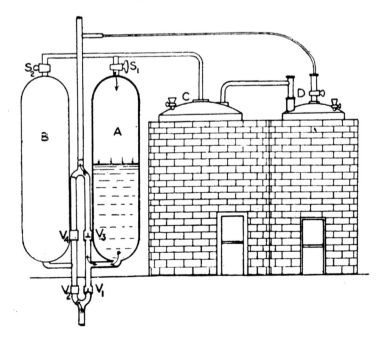

Diagram of the Savery steam engine (1698), the invention that changed the world.

"STRATA" SMITH

Like William Buckland, William Smith grew up surrounded by fossils. He was born in a rural town in Oxfordshire, the same fossil-filled county that contained the Stonesfield quarries. Smith grew up working on his uncle's dairy farm, where the local milkmaids would weigh milk using what they called "pound stones," which were so numerous that they could be found lying on the ground. They were actually fossilized sea urchins.

Unlike Buckland, however, Smith did not receive much formal education. He was a commoner. His father was a blacksmith who died when he was just 8 years old. Smith had to leave school at the age of 11 to earn money, but he continued his education on his own. The nearest bookstore was 44 miles away in Oxford. Whenever he was able, he would take the full-day journey into town to buy a textbook on a subject that interested him. He taught himself geometry, and he was about to teach himself surveying when, by pure chance, he walked out of the bookstore and ran into an engineer who noticed the surveying book under Smith's arm. He offered Smith an apprenticeship.

William Smith, geologist, 1837.

A "pound stone"/sea urchin used by Oxfordshire dairymaids for weighing milk.

Humans didn't dig into the ground looking for dinosaur bones. We dug down looking for money and power.
We dug for coal.

Smith jumped at the chance. It was a good time to be an engineer in England. Coal mining required many forms of engineering expertise, and it paid better than any job Smith could find in his rural hometown. He followed his new boss around the country, learning his trade. Once his apprenticeship was over, he was hired to work in a coal mine known as Mearns Pit. He would later refer to Mearns as the "Birthplace of Geology" (Smith did not suffer from low self-esteem).

Smith had never been educated enough to read about Steno's laws of geology. But working alongside the coal miners, he learned the same lesson. The miners spent every day underground, and had become intimately familiar with its layered formation. To help themselves navigate through the mines, they even gave the layers nicknames like Rage Rock, the Race, Temple Cloud, and Kingswood Toad.

William Smith became so fascinated with these layers, which he called strata, that his friends started calling him "Strata" Smith. He traveled to several different mines, and in each one he noticed that the same strata kept repeating themselves in the exact same order.

He wanted to explore this idea even further, but that was impossible. To track the movement of dozens of underground rock layers would require something absurd like digging a massive, miles-long trench in the Earth. That's when William Smith became one of the luckiest men in the history of science. That's when England was hit by Canal Mania.

Illustration of underground miners, mid-19th century. Mine work was (and still is) hot, cramped, dangerous, and dirty.

Diagram of strata in an English coal mine
down to 70 feet. Note some of the great strata
names: black bat, soft white clunch, tender
blue bind.

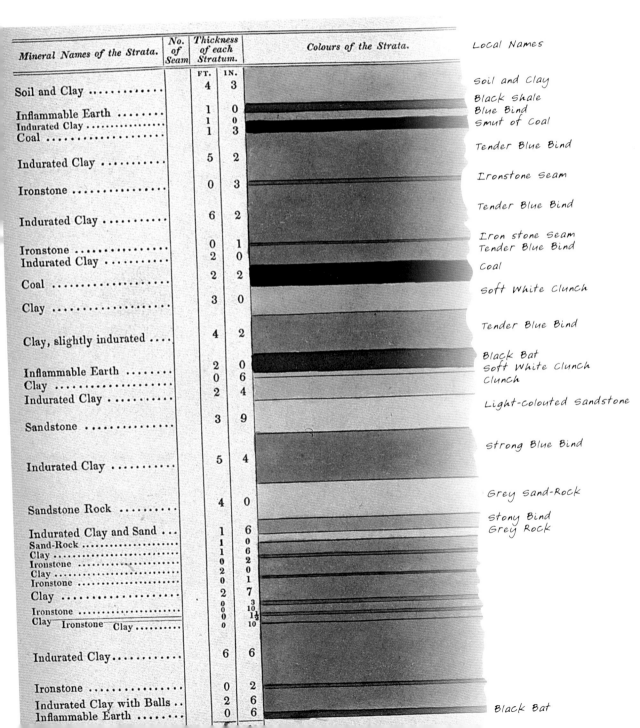

Mineral Names of the Strata.	No. of Seam	Thickness of each Stratum.		Colours of the Strata.	Local Names
		FT.	IN.		
Soil and Clay		4	3		Soil and Clay
					Black Shale
Inflammable Earth		1	0		Blue Bind
Indurated Clay		1	0		Smut of Coal
Coal		1	3		
Indurated Clay		5	2		Tender Blue Bind
Ironstone		0	3		Ironstone Seam
Indurated Clay		6	2		Tender Blue Bind
Ironstone		0	1		Iron stone Seam
Indurated Clay		2	0		Tender Blue Bind
Coal		2	2		Coal
Clay		3	0		Soft White Clunch
Clay, slightly indurated		4	2		Tender Blue Bind
Inflammable Earth		2	0		Black Bat
Clay		0	6		Soft White Clunch
Indurated Clay		2	4		Clunch
Sandstone		3	9		Light-coloured sandstone
Indurated Clay		5	4		Strong Blue Bind
Sandstone Rock		4	0		Grey Sand-Rock
Indurated Clay and Sand ...		1	6		Stony Bind
Sand-Rock		1	0		Grey Rock
Clay		1	6		
Ironstone		0	2		
Clay		2	0		
Ironstone		0	1		
Clay		2	7		
Ironstone		0	3		
Clay Ironstone Clay		0	10½		
		0	1½		
		0	10		
Indurated Clay...........		6	6		
Ironstone		0	2		
Indurated Clay with Balls ..		2	6		Black Bat
Inflammable Earth		0	6		

FOSSIL NICKNAMES

Every English child in the eighteenth and nineteenth century grew up surrounded by fossils. Fossils were so common in England that they got absorbed into local cultures and mythologies. Every area of England had different nicknames for their local fossils.

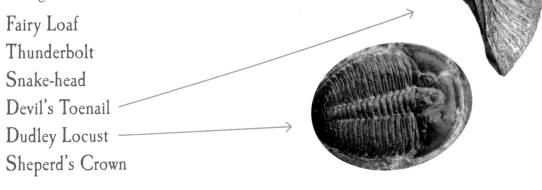

Fairy Loaf
Thunderbolt
Snake-head
Devil's Toenail
Dudley Locust
Sheperd's Crown

CANAL MANIA!

Here is an interesting engineering problem:

The coal mines of England were in the countryside, but the factories that burned the coal were in the city. And coal is heavy. By 1800, England was digging up *100 million tons* of coal every year. So how could they move something that heavy across a great distance?

Trains weren't powerful enough yet. Trucks wouldn't be invented for another century. The only option was to load those millions of tons onto wagons and make tired horses pull them along muddy country roads.

It wasn't ideal.

A solution came in 1761, when the Duke of Bridgewater built a canal that connected his mine to the city of Manchester. The coal was loaded onto floating barges and hauled by horses on the side of the canal.

It was a smashing success. With the canal, one horse could pull 400 times more coal than a packhorse. It could pull 80 times more than a wagon. It was a great solution for other goods as well. By avoiding bumpy roads, potters could ship their goods without breakage. Brewers could ship their beer without spilling.

Overnight, the duke became a rich(er) man. A canal was the key to economic prosperity. Suddenly, every city and county in England wanted a canal of its own. This inspired a period of frenzied digging known as Canal Mania.

Planning and engineering a canal is a huge endeavor. There were very few

people in England with the expertise to pull it off, so counties began hiring anyone with relevant experience. William Smith had never engineered a canal before, but digging coal mines was close enough. The county of Somerset gave Smith the money, tools, and permission to dig a network of canals through their entire county.

They may have wanted a canal, but what Smith really wanted was to satisfy his own curiosity. He wanted to slice open the countryside and look around.

This image covers almost 200 miles; however, it is just one minor detail on Smith's map. Inside the circled area is the town of Oxford. In the hills to the left is the town of Stonesfield (not pictured). It sits on top of the thin blue strata known as "Forest Marble." This formed 174–163 million years ago during the Middle Jurassic period described on the first page of this book. This is the tomb of the Megalosaurs.

Steno dissected a shark; Smith was going to dissect the planet.

THE MAP THAT CHANGED THE WORLD

So what did Smith observe during his dissection?

Exactly what he suspected. The strata he'd mapped in the mines matched the strata that ran through the entire county. The layers of rock would rise and fall in predictable patterns because *they always maintained the same order*.

It should be noted that Smith was no lone genius. In Germany, France, and North and South America, quarry and mining engineers were noticing the strata patterns in rock. The difference is that the others were distinguishing the strata by examining the mineral makeup of the rocks. Smith developed a different method that turned out to be crucial to

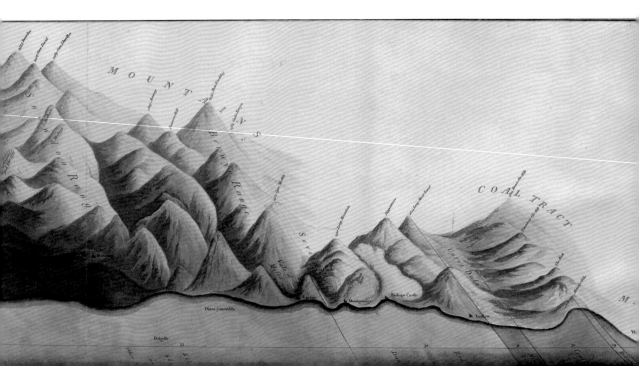

our understanding of Earth's past.

In certain places, it was hard to tell where each strata stopped and started. For instance, dark red clay right next to black coal was visually hard to tell apart. Smith soon learned that he could tell the difference by looking at the fossils. Each strata contained completely different types of fossils.

Some strata contained land fossils like ferns and tree trunks. Some strata contained the fossils of saltwater animals, and others had fossils from freshwater animals. Sometimes these wildly different layers would be right on top of each other! More importantly, seawater shells never appeared in freshwater strata, and vice versa. Like the strata, the fossils always appeared in the same order.

Smith used these fossil patterns to map out the strata of Somerset County.

When he was done with the canal, his ambition grew. He decided to create what his biographer would later call "the map that changed the world." It was the first attempt to create a geological (strata) map of an entire country. The culmination of the efforts of the World Makers, Steno, and Hutton, Smith's map was the first time that humans would have an accurate picture of the planet we live on.

His quest took 14 years as he traveled and single-handedly studied 50,000 square miles of England. During this time, he didn't just analyze the land; he began to analyze fossils as well. He visited as many collections as he could find. He dug up fossils, secured invitations to aristocrats' homes so he could view their cabinets of curiosities, and eventually (inevitably) he visited one of the finest fossil sites in all of England—the town of Lyme Regis.

GEOLOGICAL SECTION FROM LONDON TO SNOWDON,

SHOWING THE VARIETIES OF THE STRATA, AND THE CORRECT ALTITUDES OF THE HILLS.

by William Smith Civil Engineer
1817

Coloured to correspond with his

Geological Map of England and Wales.

The Numbers refer to the Geological Table by the same Author.

There, Smith visited the same beach that the Bucklands walked every weekend. It was 1794, and William Buckland would have been 10 years old. Perhaps young William even passed Smith and watched as the older man made sketches of the layers of the cliffs. They would eventually meet 15 years later, and Buckland would ultimately help to save Smith's life. But in 1794, Buckland was just another of the many Lyme Regis children fossil hunting along the beach.

After two more years of travel and study, in 1796, Smith wrote down the thoughts he'd been forming since the Somerset Canal. It was a particularly cold and windy day that forced Smith out of his usual research in the fields and into a pub called the Swan Inn. There, next to a crackling fire and with some time on his hands, he wrote in his journal:

Fossils have long been studied as great curiosities . . . showed and admired with as much pleasure as a child's rattle or hobby-horse . . . this has been done by thousands who have never paid the least regard to that wonderful order . . . which Nature has . . . assigned to each class its particular stratum.

He wrote: *"It is the pattern that is everything."*

THE PATTERNS OF TIME

Like Steno's illustrations of how Earth forms in layers, Smith's "pattern" doesn't seem like much at first, but it's one of the great keys to the discovery of dinosaurs.

Smith now understood that the strata and their fossils were telling a story: At different points in the history of the planet, Britain had been covered by the ocean, then freshwater like rivers and lakes, then dry land, then ocean again, and on and on into the past.

As he traveled, Smith got even better at

Kuo

In 1080 A.D., *over 700 years earlier*, a Chinese scholar named Shen Kuo made exactly the same observations as Steno, Hutton, and Smith combined. A landslide revealed an underground forest of petrified bamboo (in an area where bamboo could not normally grow due to the wrong climate). Kuo decided that the planet must have once had an entirely different climate, and the area was slowly covered by layers of river soil. He noted all of this in his book, *The Dream Pool Essays*. However, he fell out of favor with the Chinese emperor and his ideas were suppressed.

> **"All the fossils that we have ever found have always been found in the appropriate place in the time sequence. There are no fossils in the wrong place."**
>
> —RICHARD DAWKINS,
> EVOLUTIONARY BIOLOGIST

recognizing the strata and fossil patterns. He was able to point to distant mountains that he had never visited before and declare what sort of shells could be found at their peaks. And he was right.

One time, a group of friends scattered fossils on a table and bet that he couldn't arrange them in the exact order they were found underground. He did, and he was right.

By becoming an expert on the geology of England, Smith had accidentally made himself an expert on its fossils. The strata weren't just showing the history of Earth. *They were showing the history of life on Earth!*

Smith was so single-minded in the creation of his geological map that he didn't pursue the question that naturally springs out of this idea. It is the final,

and most important, question to be answered before humans could discover dinosaurs.

Why did each strata start and stop? If each strata represented an entire era of Earth's history, what caused these eras to come to an end? Most importantly, what happened to the animals who were alive when the end came?

Leo
Leonardo da Vinci—inventor, engineer, and painter of the *Mona Lisa* and *The Last Supper*—observed fossilized clamshells on mountains and guessed *all* of it correctly—extinct animals, strata, and time periods of Earth.

However, Leonardo only wrote his ideas in his notebooks, which he kept a closely guarded secret. He even wrote backward to help disguise his ideas in case anyone did manage to get a glimpse inside.

The examples of both da Vinci and Shen Kuo demonstate the importance of one of science's most basic principles: If you don't record your observations and pass it on to others, then your knowledge dies with you. This book started with Steno, Hooke, and Plot because they recorded their observations, creating the first links in a chain of ideas. *That* is science.

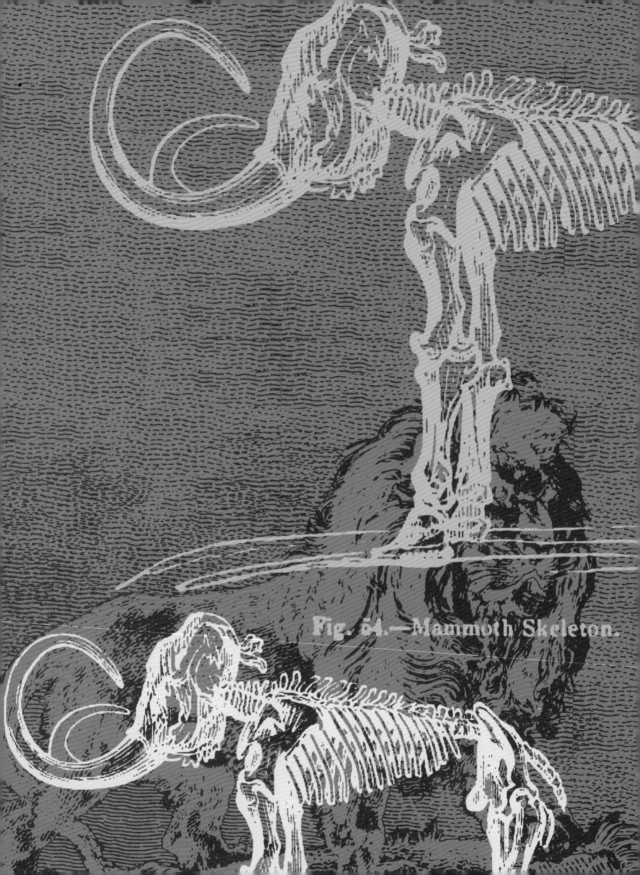

Fig. 54.—Mammoth Skeleton.

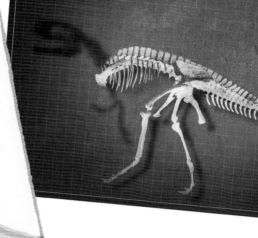

PART 6
REVOLUTION

THE SIX BLIND MEN & THE ELEPHANT
PART 2

The beginning of this book told the story of the Six Blind Men and the Elephant. Each blind man guessed at the true nature of an elephant based on their limited ability to see. Then, someone came along and united all of their ideas with his vision. He saw the whole elephant.

In the history of dinosaurs (and all extinct animals), the man with vision was Georges Cuvier. In the scientific Hall of Fame, certain names are well known— Isaac Newton, Louis Pasteur, Albert Einstein. Cuvier's name is usually left out, but it shouldn't be.

In order to discover dinosaurs, the single biggest piece of the puzzle was the idea that animals could go extinct. If animals could go extinct, then the mystery of strange bones found underground isn't so mysterious. They simply belong to an animal never seen by humans.

Cuvier was the person who proved the idea of extinction, and he did it by finding an elephant.

Literally.

GOD IS DEAD

Much of the action in this book is centered around England, but in truth, a great deal of thinking, digging, and discovery was happening all over Europe. Each country had a different history and culture that affected how their scientists viewed the world, and gave them a different perspective.

One of the most powerful ideas holding back the discovery of dinosaurs (and all other extinct animals) was the Christian idea that a perfect, loving, all-powerful

God would not let one of his creatures die. But in 1793, something occurred that radically altered the thinking of everyone who lived in the country of France.

PARIS, FRANCE
JANUARY 21, 1793

Louis XVI, the king of France, stepped into a carriage with a priest and two guards. In front of the carriage were soldiers on horseback and a troupe of drummers. They rolled through the Paris streets to the beat of the drummers, who alerted the public to make way, make way for the king. Finally the carriage arrived at a massive town square. It was filled with an estimated 20,000 people, but a row of cannons held them back from the center of the square.

The carriage pulled into the clearing, and the king stepped out. The crowd strained forward to get a better view. Very few ordinary citizens had ever seen the king before, much less been this close to him. The kings of Europe who had ruled their countries for thousands of years were not ordinary humans. They were seen as divine messengers, chosen by God.

The people watched as their god-king climbed up onto a platform that had been specially built in his honor. It was a guillotine.

King Louis XVI was there to die.

He began to address the crowd, but his speech was cut short by a soldier who ordered the drums to roll. Then, King Louis XVI placed his head beneath the guillotine . . .

. . . and the blade dropped.

Reports from the time all agree that what followed was a deep, stunned silence. No one had ever seen a god executed before. Then, the youngest soldier on the platform, an 18-year-old new recruit, picked up the head of their former god-king and showed it to the crowd. He used the head to make rude gestures, and the crowd started to laugh.

The silence broke. Several people began to shout, *"Vive la République!"* ("Long live the Republic!")

Until that point in history, the phrase shouted in the presence of the king was, *"Vive le roi!"* ("Long live the king!") But the king was dead. A new form of government would now take his place—a people's Republic. The entire crowd of 20,000 people took up the chant: "Long live the Republic!"

Women rushed forward and dipped their handkerchiefs in the pool of blood spreading out from the king's headless corpse. This was the French Revolution, and it demonstrated how an entire era of history—thousands of years—can suddenly end—swiftly, and with violence.

THE CABINETS THROWN OPEN!

The French Revolution opened the floodgates of fossil research. Tormented by

years of poverty and famine, the people of France swarmed over the king's properties around the country, taking it all in the name of the people. This included the king's personal wonder rooms.

Ruling over large portions of the world for generations meant the kings of France had acquired enough curiosities to fill entire buildings. The name given to these buildings was Le Jardin royal des Plantes ("the Royal Garden of Plants"). After the Revolution, it was renamed the France National Museum of Natural History. It was no longer the king's personal museum; it was now a public institution. It still stands at the same address today.

The Revolution didn't stop there. The public was determined to destroy the entire French aristocracy. They looted their castles, and alongside the fine clothes, fine wines, and furniture, they found well-stocked cabinets of curiosities. Not knowing what to do with these fossils, they shipped them off to the new museum of natural history in Paris.

On top of that, a series of wars broke

The former wonder room of the king, now the France National Museum of Natural History.

It was an unprecedented avalanche of information. No human had ever viewed, processed, and sorted that many fossils before. Most people would have been overwhelmed by the task, but it all landed on the desk of a young man who had just started his job as a lowly museum assistant. This was Georges Cuvier and, fortunately, he was one of the great geniuses in the history of science.

"A PEARL IN THE DUNGHILL"

Cuvier's intelligence was obvious to everyone from the time he was a child. He had learned to read by the age of four. As a teenager, he learned to speak German fluently within a year. His parents had high hopes that he would become a priest . . . but then Georges met the World Makers.

out between the new Republic of France and the other monarchies of Europe. Whenever French soldiers captured a foreign town, they would ransack it and ship home anything of value—art, jewels, and fossils. This is a good indication of how far the thinking on fossils had progressed in the last 100 years. Soldiers considered fossils to be as valuable as art and jewels. During these wars, approximately 150 wooden crates of fossils came streaming into the museum of natural history.

The young Georges Cuvier.

Count de Buffon (the one, you may remember, who heated balls of metal to determine the age of Earth) was the leading naturalist in France at the time. He wrote a massive, best-selling book titled *Natural History*. In it, Buffon didn't just relate his theory of Earth's origins, he included illustrations and descriptions of every animal (both domestic and exotic) known at the time.

That book changed Cuvier's life. He fell wildly in love with natural history. He read and studied anatomy on his own. However, Cuvier was from the sleepy, rural Jura region of France. Both geographically and culturally, it was a long way from the scientific community in Paris.

As a country boy, Cuvier had no connections to the big city, no way to advance his position in life. After his schooling, he took a job tutoring the children of aristocrats, and that's probably where he would have remained if it hadn't been for a bizarre quirk of fate.

One evening, Cuvier happened to attend a lecture by a traveling physician. What no one knew was this physician was actually a famous scientist (and aristocrat) named Tessier, in disguise. He was on the run.

After the French Revolution came a time known as the Terror. The death of King Louis XVI had given the mobs of Paris a taste for blood. They rounded up hundreds of aristocrats and sent them to the guillotine. The remaining aristocrats, like Tessier, feared the same fate and fled into the countryside. To earn money (his fortune had been confiscated), Tessier began giving a series of lectures.

Cuvier was a fan of Tessier's writing, and during the lecture, he saw through the disguise. When Cuvier addressed Tessier by his proper name, the terrified man cried: "I am known then! And consequently lost!"

A page from the book that changed Cuvier's life, Buffon's *Natural History*.

Jurassic Origins

It's one of the quirky coincidences in science history: Cuvier, the man most responsible for the discovery of dinosaurs, was born in the same area that gave its name to the most famous era of dinosaurs—the Jurassic era.

The Jura Mountains cover approximately 225 miles of eastern France. "Jura" means "wooded," so called because the forests that cluster on this mountain range are so dense and numerous.

In 1795, a geologist/naturalist named Alexander Von Humboldt realized that the hills of Jura, France, were made of a unique layer of limestone that wasn't on any geological map. So he named it Jurassic rock. Little did he know that this limestone strata was formed in the time that some of the most recognizable dinosaurs in history were alive—*Megalosaurus*, *Stegosaurus*, and *Brachiosaurus*. The Jurassic rock gave its name to the Jurassic era.

"No," said Cuvier, "you are henceforth the object of our most anxious care."

Cuvier protected Tessier, and the two struck up a friendship. Tessier was so grateful that he recommended Cuvier to his contacts in Paris (and revealed his true thoughts about life in the countryside) when he wrote: "I have just found a pearl in the dunghill of Normandy."

So in 1795, two years after the death of the king, Cuvier moved to Paris and became an assistant in anatomy at the National Museum of Natural History. He was just 25 years old.

THE PATTERNS OF PARTS

When Cuvier began his job at the museum, paleontology (the study of life in Earth's past) did not yet exist. He would invent it a year later.

If you wanted to train the perfect paleontologist, you would give him or her Cuvier's job. He was working with the largest collections of fossils ever assembled.

As fossils poured into the France National Museum of Natural History, he had to catalogue and file away every one. To do that, he had to identify what sort of animal each fossil came from, often working from only small fragments of bone. We can only imagine how frustrating that was since many of these bones belonged to animals that no longer existed. However, Cuvier noticed that fossilized bones followed the same rules as modern bones.

As Cuvier sifted through mountains of fossils, like William Smith, he began to recognize patterns that no one had seen before. While Smith's patterns were based on geology, Cuvier's were based on anatomy. He developed a theory he called "the correlation of parts."

The basis of this idea is that most animals (including humans) are symmetrical. That means one side will match the other, more or less. So if one femur (thighbone) is found, an anatomist can guess that the animal's other femur (or other three, if it's a four-legged animal) will have a similar weight and length.

On the other hand, an animal with a 5-pound body can't have a 20-pound skull. It wouldn't be able to hold up its head. An animal with a foot that is 2 feet long won't be 2 feet tall. It wouldn't be able to walk.

"The correlation of parts," however, is far more precise. Consider the human body: A human's arm span (from fingertip to fingertip) almost exactly matches the person's height. Your forearm and foot are the same length. The length of your femur bone is one-quarter the size of your height. By looking at even a single thighbone, an anatomist can reconstruct an entire human skeleton.

The more Cuvier studied animals, the more patterns he noticed. A skull with canine teeth will come from a predator.

They need those teeth to tear into meat. An animal with hooves and horns will always be an herbivore. That also means it will have molar teeth for grinding up plants. It will have eyes on the side of its head, since herbivores are animals of prey and need better peripheral vision to watch for predators.

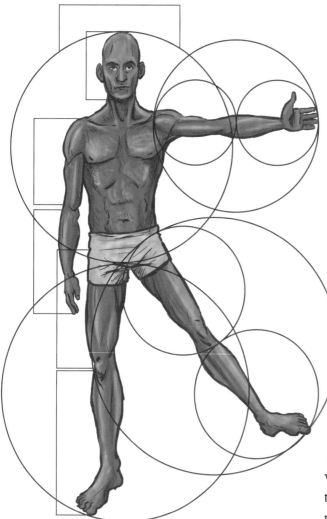

"As Cuvier could correctly describe a whole animal by the contemplation of a single bone, so the observer who has thoroughly understood one link in a series of incidents should be able to accurately state all the other ones, both before and after."

—SHERLOCK HOLMES,

THE FIVE ORANGE PIPS

Within a short period of time, Cuvier got very, very good at his job. He became famous at parties for being able to identify an animal from a single bone. Cuvier's method and incredible forensic abilities helped inspire the creation of the character Sherlock Holmes.

Cuvier had been working at the museum for less than a year when he was told he would have to give an educational lecture to the public. Cuvier would not have been nervous, though. He was known to have a very high opinion of himself. Besides, he knew what he wanted to talk about.

Over the last year, he had developed a theory about the mysterious fossils that he couldn't identify. Before Cuvier, several naturalists and philosophers had examined fossilized bones and guessed that those animals no longer existed, but they had no way to prove it. None of them had access to a king's collection. But Cuvier did. And he was certain that, buried deep in the museum, he had found the proof.

Cuvier was going to talk about elephants.

A NEW ELEPHANT

Elephants were not the total curiosity they were in Dr. Plot's day. King Louis XVI received elephants as gifts from his colonies every year and displayed them publicly. However, they were still rare enough that no one was able to compare and contrast elephants from different parts of the world. To the public, all elephants looked alike.

Cuvier had an advantage that most people did not. Like Steno staring into the mouth of a dead great white shark, Cuvier was able to study the teeth of an elephant up close. Among the bones that came into the museum were the skulls of two modern elephants—one from Sri Lanka and the other from South Africa.

On April 4, 1796, Cuvier stood in front of a crowded lecture hall and began by telling his audience that an elephant from Asia and an elephant from Africa are two entirely separate species. "The elephant from [Sri Lanka] differs more from that of Africa than the horse from the ass or the goat from the sheep."

How did he know? It was the teeth.

Cuvier noted that the Sri Lankan elephant's molar teeth had wavy ridges on the surface "like festooned ribbons." The African elephant, on the other hand, had teeth with ridges in the shape of diamonds. Because of their different environments and different diets, each elephant had evolved a completely different set of teeth (although the idea of evolution was still several decades away). This speech by Cuvier marked the moment that humans began to distinguish between the African and Asian elephant. The identification of two distinct species would be enough to cement the reputation of most scientists, but Cuvier was just getting started.

Now, he told the audience, let us examine another set of teeth. Cuvier then held up a fossilized tooth that was the size of a brick and weighed five pounds. It had traveled a long way to get to Paris.

THE OHIO ANIMAL

Thirty years earlier, in North America, a group of French soldiers wanted to launch a sneak attack on British forces by sailing boats down the Ohio River. They hired warriors from the Canadian Abenaki tribe to be their river guides. Halfway through their journey, the Abenaki went hunting for food, but when they came back, their canoes were filled with bones.

Massive, fossilized bones. A femur as tall as a man. Great tusks of fossilized ivory. And the tooth that Cuvier held up in the lecture hall.

The Abenaki had stumbled onto one of North America's greatest fossil sites, the marsh now known as Big Bone Lick, in the state of Kentucky. The Abenaki retrieved them because they believed fossils brought good luck, but the French soldiers saw them as a gift fit for their king. They shipped the bones off to Paris, where they became the first fossils sent from the New World.

No one could identify these mystery bones with a living creature so they simply called it the "Ohio Animal." They filed it away in the king's wonder rooms, where it sat unnoticed for thirty years, until Cuvier spotted it.

In addition to the "Ohio Animal" tooth, Cuvier found a similar tooth from the other side of the planet, in Siberia.

By their shape, size, and the tusks that were found with them, it's obvious that these teeth belonged to creatures related to the elephant. But using the same logic that was applied to the Asian and African elephants, the teeth showed that there was a difference.

The Siberian "elephant" had flat teeth, to help it grind the grass that grew in the Siberian grasslands. The Ohio Animal had molars with round bulges that made it stronger and more robust. Those helped it chomp the tree branches and shrubs found in the swamps of Kentucky. In each case, their teeth were totally unique.

Therefore, said Cuvier, there was only one conclusion. These fossilized teeth belonged to elephant-like animals that were different from modern elephants "as much as, or more than, the dog differs from the jackal." He called the Siberian elephant a "mammoth." The Ohio Animal was renamed "mastodon."

But, Cuvier asked the audience, "what has become of these two enormous animals of which one no longer finds any living traces?"

Cuvier's sketch of the Ohio Animal/mastodon molar (right) and the Siberian mammoth's molar (left). Note how different the surfaces are.

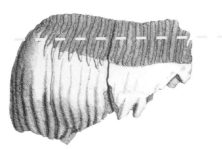

Cuvier had concentrated his efforts on the Ohio Animal for a reason. Smaller creatures like ammonites might be extinct, but scientists couldn't be sure. Ammonites were so small that they might exist *somewhere*, but simply hadn't been found yet. Elephants, on the other hand, are the largest land animal in the world. If mastodons were still alive, someone would have seen them by now.

When Thomas Jefferson sent the explorers Lewis and Clark across the continent of North America, one of his main goals was to find a living mastodon. They found nothing. Because of Cuvier, people now understood why. It had gone extinct.

Previous generations had resisted the idea. They believed that God had created all animals, and nothing divine could just suddenly die. But Cuvier was a product of the French Revolution. His job, his museum, and all of his fossils had come to him because of the sudden and violent death of the divine King Louis XVI. The people of France knew from firsthand experience that an entire era could end with the drop of a guillotine blade. Not only that, but after the Revolution, the church in France (which was closely tied to the king) lost much of its power and was unable to enforce its ideas.

Cuvier was free to think anything he

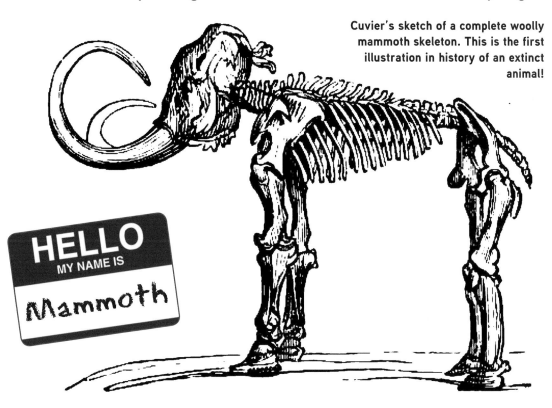

Cuvier's sketch of a complete woolly mammoth skeleton. This is the first illustration in history of an extinct animal!

HELLO
MY NAME IS
Mammoth

BREAST-TOOTH

At a certain point, Cuvier realized that the name "Ohio Animal" was unwieldy. He needed something to replace it. He noted that the bumps on its molar teeth looked like breasts. So he combined the Greek words for "breast" (*mastos*) and "tooth" (*odont*), and came up with the name "mastodon."

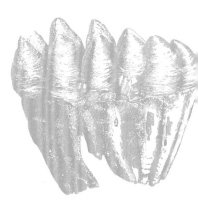

• •

wanted without fear of persecution, and he had no problem believing that extinction could wipe out previous life on Earth. Every era, he believed, ended sud-denly and violently in "revolutions that were so stupendous that . . . the thread of Nature's operations was broken.

"All of these facts," he declared at the end of his speech, "seem to me to prove the existence of a world previous to ours, destroyed by some kind of catastrophe."

These catastrophes, he said, were "a revolution of the globe."

"A WORLD PREVIOUS TO OURS"

For thousands of years, the world beneath our feet was a mystery-box, full of curiosities that made no sense. The idea of extinction was the key. Now that the box was unlocked, entire herds

REVOLUTION!

In 1962, a science historian named Thomas Kuhn wrote a book titled *The Structure of Scientific Revolutions*. To explain how scientific revolutions occur, he popularized the idea of "a paradigm" (pronounced: para-dime).

A paradigm is a theory, or way of thinking, that we use to explain the world. However, there are sometimes discrepancies or irregularities that the paradigm can't explain (seashells on a mountaintop, for example). When enough of these irregularities build up, it means that the paradigm itself is flawed.

Scientific revolutions occur when someone (a scientist, philosopher, historian) creates a new paradigm, an entirely new way of thinking, that explains everything, including the irregularities.

A few examples of these revolutions/paradigm shifts are Copernicus realizing the Earth revolves around the sun, Einstein and the theory of relativity, and most importantly for this book, Cuvier proving the existence of extinction.

of long-lost animals came rushing out. The mastodon and mammoth were just the beginning. In that same year, Cuvier received a set of meticulous fossil illustrations from scientists in Madrid, Spain. The drawings were of strange, massive bones found in South America.

Working only from these illustrations, Cuvier used his "correlation of parts" to piece together the bones, deduce what was missing, and figure out what the assembled animal would have looked like. When he finished, he had created an animal unlike anything anyone had ever seen.

It was a 4-ton, 20-foot-long, 12-foot-tall ground sloth, with claws so large that the beast was nicknamed "Great Claw."

"Would it not also be glorious for man to burst the limits of time, and, by means of observations, to ascertain the history of this world?"

—CUVIER, 1813

Cuvier decided to name it *Megatherium* (Greek for "great beast"). Even today,

Cuvier's reconstruction of the elephant-sized *Megatherium.*

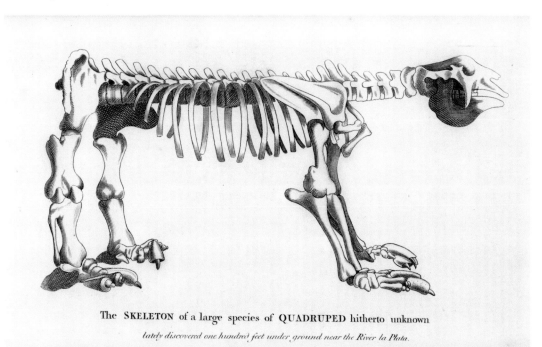

The SKELETON of a large species of QUADRUPED hitherto unknown
lately discovered one hundred feet under ground near the River la Plata.

PLATE IX.

CERVUS MEGACEROS,
ISLE OF MAN OR IRISH ELK.
Royal Museum. College. Edinburgh.

Cuvier's illustration of *Megaloceros*, also known as "the Irish Elk." It stood approx. 7 feet tall with antlers 12 feet across!

Megatherium ranks as one of the largest land mammals on record. We now know that it lived from 5 million to 10,000 years ago, and it was most likely hunted into extinction by early humans.

Cuvier's immediate success in discovering a new extinct species inspired him. He sent out a public notice for amateurs and enthusiasts to send him their fossils for identification. As the donations poured in, he took charge of an entire wing at the museum. Visitors were astonished to find that his office was actually a hallway with 11 desks lined up end to end. Each desk was covered with the partially reconstructed skeleton of some fantastical animal from the past.

There was *Megaloceros*, a 7-foot-tall elk that had antlers 12 feet wide. There was a pygmy hippopotamus, a prehistoric cave bear, and 6 species of deerlike creatures that lived around Paris. Within the first 4 years of his lecture, Cuvier identified 23 extinct species!

Through his popular public lectures, Cuvier became a larger-than-life celebrity, in several senses of the term. The endless hours of work and his love of food caused him to become so fat that he earned the nickname "Mastodon." But the most famous French novelist at the time, Honoré de Balzac, marveled at Cuvier's seemingly magical abilities:

"Is not Cuvier the greatest poet of our century? [He] has reconstructed worlds from a whitened bone; rebuilt . . . cities from a tooth."

By 1812, Cuvier had identified 49 extinct animals. Even Cuvier himself seemed astonished at how fast it all happened. He wrote: "If so many lost species have been restored in so little time, how many must . . . exist still in the depths of Earth?"

The underworld constantly surprised him. All of his initial discoveries were mammals. They all looked somewhat similar to modern animals. But as miners and quarrymen dug deeper into Earth (and deeper into the past), the bones became stranger and stranger.

THE REPTILE LAYERS

In 1801, Cuvier received an illustration of a bizarre fossil from a cabinet of curiosities in Germany.

The first naturalists to look at the tangled bones focused on the long arms and fingers and decided that they must be the fins of some sea creature. To their surprise, Cuvier disagreed. Despite the fact that no similar animals existed as a model for his idea, Cuvier insisted that this creature's arms were actually wings. It was a flying reptile.

He gave it the name "wing fingered," or *Pterodactylus*. This was the first time anyone had identified an extinct species of reptile. It wasn't the last, and it certainly wasn't the weirdest.

In 1808, he began to study the skull of the Meuse monster.

The legend of the Meuse monster was known throughout Europe. Around 1770 in the Netherlands, workers digging in an underground cavern uncovered a skull unlike anything anyone had ever seen. It had a long, pointed jaw with

Illustration of the first pterodactyl.

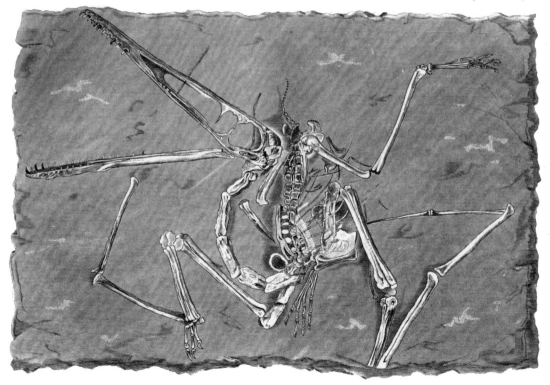

sharp, shark-like teeth. It was so large it required several men to carry it.

Not knowing what else to call it, the villagers simply named it after the nearby Meuse River. The news of this "Meuse monster" spread across Europe. It became an object of desire. So when a war broke out between the Netherlands and France in 1794, a French official ordered soldiers to seize the famous skull and bring it back to France.

However, when French troops entered the town, they found that the villagers had hidden the skull. The French searched for it without success until finally, legend has it, they offered 600 bottles of wine as a reward to the person who brought it to them.

It turned out 600 bottles of wine was the correct price for a monster skull. Skull and wine were exchanged the next day, and the skull was shipped off to France's National Museum of Natural History.

Many speculated that the Meuse mon-

The legend of the "Meuse monster" spread quickly around Europe. This illustration is taken from a German children's book in 1798. It shows miners excavating its skull from underground caverns in Maastricht, Netherlands.

ster was related to a crocodile, or perhaps it was some form of toothy whale. After a great deal of study, Cuvier (correctly) described it as a marine reptile and estimated its size at 50 feet long! It was later dubbed *Mosasaurus*.

Again, this would be enough to cement the reputation of any scientist, but Cuvier made one more incredibly important contribution to his field. He had teamed up with French geologists who were exploring the same ideas as William Smith:

Each strata of Earth was a separate era in Earth's history.

Each strata contained its own unique fossils.

By connecting his extinct animals with the strata in which they were found, Cuvier was taking the logical next step from Smith's ideas. Cuvier was uncovering the history of life on Earth.

"It will strike terror into your soul to see many millions of years, many thousands of races forgotten by the feeble memory of mankind . . . and whose piles of ashes on the surface of our globe form the two feet of soil which gives us our bread and flowers."

—HONORÉ DE BALZAC

The strata that contained these reptiles were *below* the strata that contained mammals. Not only that, no mammal's fossils could be found in the reptile strata.

> Not only was there a world previous to humans, there was a world previous to mammals as well.

At the beginning of the nineteenth century, the only clues we had to a pre-mammal world were a pterodactyl and a mosasaur. But what did the rest of that world look like? What else was hidden down there?

Even Cuvier didn't know. No human had ever traveled that far back into the past.

In the sixteenth century, when sailors drew up maps of the seas, they would often include entire areas that were unexplored and unknown. They began a practice of drawing mythical sea serpents in these areas and writing the words "Here Be Dragons."

The same could be said for the unknown world beneath the surface of Earth. But a whole new generation of scientists was now armed with Cuvier's ideas. They were ready to enter the unknown and hunt for dragons.

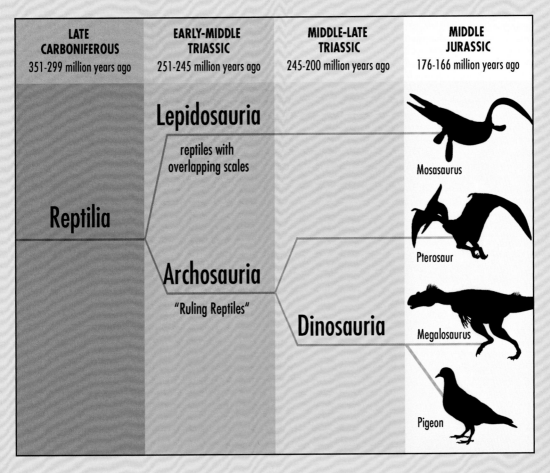

LATE CARBONIFEROUS 351-299 million years ago	EARLY-MIDDLE TRIASSIC 251-245 million years ago	MIDDLE-LATE TRIASSIC 245-200 million years ago	MIDDLE JURASSIC 176-166 million years ago

Lepidosauria

reptiles with overlapping scales

Mosasaurus

Reptilia

Archosauria

"Ruling Reptiles"

Pterosaur

Dinosauria

Megalosaurus

Pigeon

DINOSAUR, DEFINED

Considering this book is called *The First Dinosaur*, it might feel like we've reached the end with the discovery of a pterodactyl and a mosasaur. Like dinosaurs, these were awesome, extinct reptile creatures that lived (and died) around the same time as each other. *Mosasaurus* is especially confusing, since its name sounds so dinosaur-y.

BUT . . . a "dinosaur" is a specific class of creature. To group a class of species together, biologists look into the evolutionary history of these creatures to see what anatomical parts they have in common. As you can see from the evolution chart above, a megalosaur has more in common with a pigeon than with a mosasaur or pterosaur.

Dinosaurs are currently defined by a system known as "cladism," which groups species by their shared evolutionary history. Cladism shows that the one characteristic all dinosaurs have in common is a hole in the hip socket where the back leg joins the body (the technical term for this hole is the "perforate acetabulum"). For more on this, see "Joined at the Hip" on page 181.

Professor Leonard Finkelman, a philosopher of science, describes it like this: "If you think that *T. rex* is a dinosaur and *Triceratops* is a dinosaur and *Diplodocus* is a dinosaur, then the only thing that all dinosaurs actually have in common is a hole in their hip sockets. But birds have the same hole in their hip sockets, so all birds are dinosaurs, too."

PART 7

THE DRAGON HUNTERS

CAST OF CHARACTERS

By 1808, this is what we knew:

- Earth's past is far older than human existence.

- The fossils in the ground are the record of that past.

- Animals existed in the past that do not exist now.

- Before mammals existed, there were reptiles that didn't look anything like what we see today.

Humans had all of the intellectual tools required to discover dinosaurs. All they had to do was find the right fossils.

Now consider the sort of person it took to be a nineteenth-century English fossil hunter:

These were not quarry workers who happened to come across fossils in the course of their regular jobs. These were not curiosity collectors looking for a few trinkets on a pleasant weekend afternoon.

To be a true fossil hunter meant spending hours a day, every day, for weeks on end in places most people avoid—quarries, mines, damp caves, open fields, sea cliffs pounded by freezing waves. Fossil hunters all over the world endure these conditions, but the English were a particularly hardy breed. Rain was a constant, sunshine a luxury.

To dig a fossil out of a rock (*chip-chip-chip*) is a painfully slow, dull, physically tiring process that requires immense (*chip-chip-chip*) patience. One mishandled swing of a hammer (*WHACK!*) can destroy a fossil that had survived for 100 million years until you came along. (This happens quite frequently even today. Paleontologists sometimes joke that "Glue is a paleontologist's best friend.")

teenth century did not fit in to normal society. They were outsiders.

Even today, there are only a handful of people working at the outer edges of any particular field of science. They all know each other and compare ideas. Some are friends, some are bitter rivals, some are

> "The worse the country, the more tortured it is by water and wind, the more broken and carved, the more it attracts fossil hunters, who depend on the planet to open itself to us."
>
> —HOW TO BUILD A DINOSAUR, JACK HORNER

It then takes endless hours to clean, assemble, and analyze those fossils—bent over a table, sifting through even the smallest bones in search of . . . something. Since the fossil hunters were on the frontier of discovery, they never knew exactly what they were looking for.

On top of that, *very few people actually understood what fossil hunters were doing*. Cuvier was popular in France, but because of a war between France and England, only a few English academics had read his books. Only a few knew that the history of the world had changed. To the general public, the fossil hunters were people who spent hours in the rain literally staring at rocks.

In other words, the sort of person who became a fossil hunter in the early nine-

looking for fame and fortune, and all are hoping to leave their mark on history.

The story of dinosaur discovery is no different. Only a small group of characters play a part in the final chapter of this detective story, and they all had very distinct roles:

Georges Cuvier
    —*the godlike inspiration*.
William Buckland
    —*the enthusiastic, eccentric professor*.
William Conybeare
    —*the quiet reverend*.
The quarrymen
    —*the overlooked workers*.
Mary Anning
    —*the tough-as-nails, self-educated businesswoman*.

Gideon Mantell
—*the brilliant, ambitious country doctor.*
Richard Owen
—*the man gone mad with power.*

THE NEW BREED

In 1807, a group of well-to-do men gathered in London for a dinner that was the first meeting of England's Geological Society, the first (and now oldest) organization dedicated to the study of geology. The group was made up of four doctors, three chemists, two booksellers, one minister, and only one working mineralogist.

There was one obvious candidate who wasn't invited. Despite the fact that he knew more about the geology of England than any other man alive, William "Strata" Smith was too crude, too common to fit in well with the other, more aristocratic members.

While there is no doubting the enthusiasm that the Geological Society had for their mission, there was some doubt about their ability. The curator of the society's museum called the members "a band of busy, jealous, active and revengeful witlings." And the head of the society, George Greenough, was "a charlatan and a blockhead."

This was a bit harsh, but by the time the society was formed, it was already old-fashioned. William Smith had showed

We are forming a little talking geological dinner club, of which I hope you will be a member.

that the way forward in geology wasn't talking, but getting into the field and doing the work.

When Greenough learned about William Smith's efforts to map England, he realized that the Geological Society needed a map of its own. (In fact, there is good reason to believe that the society's members actually visited Smith's printer and stole some of his ideas.)

"The theory of geology was in possession of one class of men [the wealthy], the practice in another."

—WILLIAM SMITH

To re-create Smith's research, the society needed people who were willing to do the dirty work. This marked a generational shift in English geology. The original members of the society were wealthy gentlemen who would spend occasional weekends out in the field. At Oxford, however, there were a couple of young, able-bodied students who were ready to get down and dirty.

In fact, in the entire history of science, *no one* enjoyed getting dirty more than William Buckland.

"BRETHREN OF THE HAMMER"

William Buckland loved working in the dirt, smelling dirt, and even eating it. One evening, his carriage got lost in the fog. So he stepped out of the cab, scooped up a handful of dirt, and put it in his mouth. He confidently announced to his fellow travelers that he knew their location. It tasted like the town of Uxbridge.

He happily recalled one time when he walked into an inn with his friend, William Conybeare. They were both covered in mud after spending a day outdoors gathering specimens. They dropped their wet bags full of rocks and fossils on a table and ordered food. When the innkeeper realized they were educated gentlemen, she remarked, "Well, I never! Fancy two real gentle-

men picking up stones! What won't men do for money?"

It's telling that the innkeeper thought

TASTE TEST

Geology is one of the only sciences that actually uses "taste" as a form of testing and evidence. Different minerals have different flavors. Some are salty, some are bitter, some are creamy, etc. Geologists can quickly and easily distinguish between these minerals by giving their sample a good ol' lick.

(Left) A sketch making fun of William Buckland's eccentric "field attire" by his friend Thomas Sopwith, 1840. In Buckland's hand is the famous blue bag that he took with him everywhere. It was filled with fossils and rocks, and Buckland would punctuate every conversation by pulling out samples to prove his point. In the lower right corner is "the Nest," Buckland's custom-built carriage.

(Below) Buckland's schoolmate, best friend, and fellow geologist, William Conybeare.

OUTWARD BOUND

It's important to remember that geology and paleontology were still brand-new sciences, and the idea of doing manual labor out in a field was seen as slightly bizarre. Even as late as 1818, a friend of Buckland's, Adam Sedgwick, was named professor of geology at Cambridge University (Oxford's rival). Upon accepting the job, he confessed, "Hitherto I have never turned a stone. . . ."

they were in it for the money. She couldn't imagine any other reason grown men would be interested in rocks. William Conybeare certainly didn't need the money. He was an aristocrat, the grandson of a bishop, and educated at the finest prep schools in England. Like Buckland, Conybeare went to Oxford to become a minister, but he got swept up in the romance of geology.

The two Williams had similar backgrounds, and they became fast friends. They had both spent their entire lives sitting in classrooms, memorizing books. Then along came this new science, which allowed them (*required* them, in fact!) to go on road trips around the country.

Now, they were two young men in their early 20s, riding on horseback or in carriages over the windswept hills of Britain. Those hills, Buckland wrote, were "the records of the operations of the Almighty Author . . . written by the finger of God himself." He and Conybeare were "brethren of the hammer," living on the adrenaline rush of fresh scenery, scientific discovery, and religious wonder. Is it any wonder they loved it?

Being a fossil hunter required many different talents. Not only did you have to be a scholar, scientist, and adventurer, you had to be an accomplished artist as well. Paleontology is a very visual science. Today, scientists use photographs and X-rays to document new fossils, but in the nineteenth century, none of that was available. They had to accurately draw their discoveries in order to show others.

This talent came in handy when they got bored on trips to remote locations. They would amuse each other by drawing pictures and trading them back and forth like kids in a classroom.

They imagined playing pranks on each other.

They imagined how they would celebrate if they discovered a new species like their hero, Cuvier.

A geologist's typical day in the field, by William Buckland.

TALES FROM THE ROAD

Another of Buckland's favorite stories from the road was the time he was traveling in a carriage with a stranger. They both fell asleep, but when Buckland awoke, he discovered that a box of slugs he was carrying had opened up, and the slugs had crawled up onto the face of the sleeping stranger. Unsure what to do, Buckland simply leapt out of the carriage, and left the passenger (and the slugs) to their fate.

Buckland and Conybeare were soon the most knowledgeable geologists at Oxford, surpassing even their teachers. When they graduated, the school offered them both jobs as lecturers in geology.

Conybeare declined. He had inherited money from his family, and was able to do what he liked. As a deeply religious man, he chose to become a minister in a rural town, which would leave him enough time to pursue fossil hunting as a hobby.

Buckland, too, had earned his degree as an ordained minister, but he had no inheritance to fall back on. He needed work, and he couldn't imagine anything better than lecturing about what he called "the noble science of undergroundology." He took the job.

Before they parted ways, the two

Geology Party, by William Buckland.

friends said good-bye in the most geologist manner possible. Buckland shook Conybeare's hand and wished for his friend's new home "to be founded on a bed of elephants."

BECOMING WILLIAM BUCKLAND

William Buckland wasn't a normal teacher. Not even close.

Simply entering his lecture hall was a shock to students who were used to the formal, reserved atmosphere of nineteenth-century Oxford. "I can never forget the scene which awaited me," wrote one student. "The room . . . was filled with rocks, shells and bones in dire confusion . . . at the end was my friend in his black gown looking like a necromancer [a magician who conjures up the dead]."

When he wasn't teaching, Buckland traveled around Britain collecting samples, which he stored in his classroom. By all accounts, he was not a tidy man. Every desk, every chair in his home and his classroom was covered in skulls, animal skins, bones, and curiosities of all kinds.

> "A merrier man . . .
> I never spent an hour's
> talk with—"
>
> —NEVIL STORY MASKELYNE,
> FELLOW OXFORD PROFESSOR

His lecture style was similar to his interior decorating—chaotic and exciting. He cracked jokes, he imitated the mating calls of extinct animals, he shouted and whispered for dramatic effect, he carried a bag on his shoulder from which he pulled a steady stream of fossils. In one

William Buckland lecturing to his fellow Oxford scholars in the Ashmolean Museum. The artist has filled the room with visual references to the history of geological discovery. Above Buckland's head is William Smith's map of England. In Buckland's hand is one of the ammonites that intrigued Robert Hooke. Falling off of Buckland's famously messy desk is an illustration of Mary Anning's first complete *Ichthyosaurus* skeleton (see pages 120-121). On the ground next to an enormous ammonite is the Anning ichthyosaur head that captured the attention of all of London. On the wall to the right, above the audience's heads, are some of Cuvier's greatest discoveries. At the top are the skull and 12-foot antlers of the giant Irish Elk, *Megaloceros*. Below that is Cuvier's sketch of the first extinct animal ever discovered, the woolly mammoth. This is the exact same image you can find on page 93 of this book!

memorable lecture, to demonstrate the starchiness of certain bones, he placed a bone on his dangling tongue and left it there, flopping around, as he lisped his way through the rest of his talk.

He would do anything to liven up his talks. He held classes on a moving train (this was when trains were still very new) and talked about the geology of the land-scape rolling by. His favorite thing to do, though, was to play pranks on his students. He once gave a lecture out in a field so he could better point out the local geol-ogy. What he didn't tell his students was that while he was talking, their boots were slowly sinking into wet clay. When he finished his talk, he walked away, leaving them stuck in the mud. The true lesson was to watch your footing when working out in the field.

To students who spent their days studying the Bible, Greek, and Latin, Buckland's lectures must have sounded like science fiction. Earth, he told them, was not the egg, or pudding, or ball of fire that the World Makers imagined. Instead it was like "an apple-dumpling, the fiery froth of which fills the interior, and we have just a crust to stand on." He spoke about Cuvier's "extinct species"—mastodons and mythological monsters that had come to life.

More controversially, he promoted his belief in gap creationism. To account for the difference in the age of Earth between Ussher's 6,000 years and geologists' hundreds of thousands (if not millions), Buckland proposed that between the Bible's story of creation (Earth was made in seven days) and the story of Adam and Eve, there was a gap in the story. The Bible didn't literally say how much time passed during that gap in the story, so it could be anything up to millions of years.

Some of Buckland's colleagues cried heresy. "Was ever the Word of

God laid so deplorably . . . at the feet of an infant and precocious science?" sniped one biblical geologist. The president of Ireland's scientific body, the Royal Academy, declared these ideas "fatal" to the word of the Bible and downright immoral.

When Buckland went on a research trip to Europe, one of the older deans at Oxford remarked, "Well, Buckland has gone . . . thank God we shall hear no more about this Geology!"

It wasn't just Buckland's teachings that his colleagues found exhausting. It was his over-the-top personality. In a story familiar to teachers everywhere, Buckland soon learned that his teaching job didn't pay nearly enough money. But he quickly discovered the secret of celebrities throughout history—the more outrageous he acted, the more he got attention. The more attention he got, the more pupils sought him out for private lessons, which earned him more money. He began delib-

BLOOD OF A SAINT

While traveling, Buckland visited a cathedral that was reputedly the site of a miracle. Every day, fresh saint's blood appeared on the cathedral floor. When Buckland heard this legend, he immediately threw himself onto the cathedral ground and began licking the dark liquid. He then calmly corrected the priest. This "saint's blood" was simply bat urine.

erately flaunting the more unconventional aspects of his life.

He kept a pet bear named Tiglath that he would dress as a student and

THE HEART OF A KING

Buckland and local dignitaries were attending a formal dinner with the archbishop of York. After the meal, the archbishop passed around a gilded box in which sat his most prized possession—a dried, shriveled piece of meat about the size of a nut. This, the archbishop informed them, was the heart of Louis XIV, the Sun King of France.

To this Buckland reputedly declared: "I have eaten many strange things, but have never eaten the heart of a king before." Then he grabbed the heart and ate it.

Instead of rocking horses and water rafts, the Buckland children rode dead crocodiles.

bring to school parties where, despite being underage, Tiglath was allowed to drink alcohol. He spelled the word "GUANO" (bat feces) on his front lawn using actual bat guano (apparently to advertise a plant fertilizer he was promoting). He provided his children

with dead alligators to use as rafts when they swam in the university fountain.

It worked. Buckland's lectures became some of the most popular on campus. They were attended not only by students but also by university officials and traveling dignitaries. In 1818, William Buckland was named the *very first* professor of geology at Oxford. The school had created an entirely new subject of study just for him.

It wasn't Buckland's intention, but his enthusiasm and charismatic lectures directly benefited the building of the *Megalosaurus* skeleton.

THE FOURTH BONE

Buckland's students were mostly aristocratic young men with free time and money. In other words, people with the means to become excellent curiosity collectors. One of these students, Philip Barker Webb, entered Oxford to study law but developed a love for nature and adventure after attending Buckland's class.

Webb dedicated the rest of his life (and his large inheritance) to traveling around the world collecting specimens. He also spent time closer to home in the Stonesfield quarry, where he purchased what a semiliterate miner labeled a "grate backbone."

This is the sacrum—a section of fused vertebrae in the lower back that sits between the hips. This particular piece actually turned out to be one of the most important fossils for identifying dinosaurs as an entire class of creature (see page 181).

Webb donated it to the Ashmolean collection, where it joined Sir Pegge's jawbone. The pieces of *Megalosaurus* were beginning to add up. There was now clear evidence of a large creature trapped in the rock beneath Stonesfield.

Donations from outside collectors like this were helpful. Buckland had a small budget from the school to purchase fossils for the Ashmolean, but he had almost no money himself.

His salary was so inadequate that the school offered to give him free housing . . . on the ground floor of the Ashmolean Museum. Buckland moved into the Ashmolean and began living among the bones.

In France, Cuvier had become the epicenter of all fossil research in the country. Buckland had now unwittingly reached the same position in England. He was the most prominent authority on fossils and geology in the country.

Over the next few decades, every interesting fossil found in England would flow through William Buckland

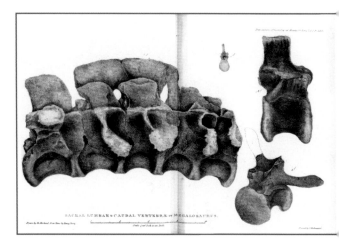

Megalosaurus **sacrum found in Stonesfield. Illustration by Mary Morland, future wife of William Buckland.**

for his advice or approval. Discoveries began to pour in from all over the British Empire, but ironically, one of the most important discoveries in the history of paleontology was a lot more local. It came from the same beach in Lyme Regis where he had spent weekends walking with his father. And it was made by the most unlikely duo—a teenage boy and his little sister.

MARY ANNING
1811

Fifteen-year-old Joseph Anning and his 12-year-old sister, Mary, were climbing over rocks along the cliffs of Lyme Regis, but they weren't there to play. Like many of the poor children in town, they were hunting for fossils to sell to tourists.

The very first fossil Mary sold was an ammonite (for the equivalent of $10). But on this particular day, Joseph spotted something in the cliff that wasn't the familiar swirl of an ammonite. This was something bigger.

It looked like part of a crocodile jaw embedded in the rocks. So he and his sister took their hammers and chisels and slowly, carefully, began to—

Chip-chip-chip-

—the fossil out of the rock. The job took months, but when they were done, they saw the four-foot-long skull of . . . well . . . *some* kind of animal. No one quite knew what.

Joseph was satisfied. Selling it would finally earn their family some real money. Mary reckoned that they might be able to find the rest of the body as well, but Joseph couldn't be bothered. Mary was only 12, but she was different. She had more patience and perseverance than most adults.

She continued searching, and almost a year later, she found it—a piece of bone buried in the cliff. So she took her rock hammer, sat down next to it, and—

Chip-chip-chip-

—she went to work. It wasn't easy work for a child, far from it. It was painful and slow and cold. Her hands hadn't yet become callused and strong. That would come later. Mary had no idea that she would be playing that tune—the ringing of her hammer on rock—for the rest of her life. But she didn't have any other choice.

Her family was hungry. They needed money.

Chip-chip-chip-

Nothing in Mary Anning's life was easy. Born into a culture

Exact replica of the Anning *Ichthyosaurus* skull as visitors to Lyme Regis would have seen it. In the background is the Lyme Regis cove.

where only men could vote, go to university, and hold political office or a professional job, Mary was a woman. Born into a society where your entire life was determined by your economic status, she grew up in crushing poverty.

Her father barely scraped out a living as a carpenter and cabinetmaker. The family lived in a house that was cheap because it was built (by accident) too close to the ocean. Waves would sometimes flood in. During one storm, the family had to leap out a window to survive.

She was one of ten children, but all of the others died except for Joseph. When she was 11, she watched her father die too, coughing himself to death from tuberculosis.

Mary Anning only had one bit of luck in her favor—she was born in Lyme Regis. By pure chance, the town of Lyme Regis lay at a crossroads of history, where many of the revolutions that formed the world came together.

One of Cuvier's catastrophes, his "revolutions of the globe," had embedded an entire ocean's worth of extinct animals in the cliffs of Lyme Regis.

The coal-burning smokestacks of the Industrial Revolution had turned England's cities into smog-filled, soot-stained, disease-ridden slums. People wanted to escape the cities to the coastal towns, where the air and water were clean.

Lyme Regis transformed from a dying fishing town into a seaside resort.

When Mary was born, England and France were at war. Travel from England to continental Europe became impossible. Upper-class tourists who would normally vacation in France or Italy traveled to England's resort towns instead. Lyme Regis became a place where the wealthy would eat, drink, and stroll in the sun by the sea. As they did, they would walk right past the Anning house. It was a poor location to live in, but an ideal spot to set up a tourist stand.

Nowadays, kids hoping to make extra money might sell lemonade. In Lyme Regis, they sold fossils.

Mary's father showed her and her brother how to find fossils along the cliffs.

The Annings (and the many other curio sellers in town) didn't actually understand what they were selling. In the early nineteenth century, commoners hadn't heard about Cuvier's extinct creatures and geology's lost worlds. So the wooden table set up outside the Annings' home advertised the bones of "croco-

Victorian women enjoying the sea breezes of Lyme Regis.

diles," "angels' wings," and "Cupid's wings."

It wasn't an easy way to make a living. Competition was fierce. One curio seller named Mr. Cruikshanks found the work so hard and the pay so small that he killed himself by leaping into the sea. Mary's father suffered a similar fate, although accidentally. While hunting for fossils, he fell from a cliff. His injuries badly affected his health. He became increasingly ill and died soon afterward. He left behind a wife, two children, and a pile of debt. The Annings were forced to apply for "poor relief." This was charity provided by the local church, a bit of bread and potatoes to prevent starvation. Children on "poor relief" like the Annings frequently suffered from malnutrition. Mary and Joseph refused to let that be their fate. They picked up the carpentry tools that their father left behind and they headed back to the same cliffs that killed him—

Chip-chip-chip-

As Mary slowly carved the "crocodile" out of the cliff, it became clear that it was far bigger than anyone had imagined. The family hired local quarry workers to carve out of the cliff the entire chunk that contained the skeleton.

This was a massive job. The block weighed several tons, and the workers had

ENDLESS HOURS

Modern paleontologists can clean fossils much faster than in the nineteenth century. They use acid, which quickly washes away limestone but leaves the fossil intact. They have air pens, which can strike the rock thousands of times an hour. Using the hand tools available in the early nineteenth century (a simple hammer and chisel) was incredibly labor intensive. But Mary was forced to work with whatever tools she could find, like the builder's trowel below.

Chris Andrew, a fossil hunter at the Lyme Regis Museum, estimates that cleaning an ichthyosaur the size of Mary's would take 8,000- 10,000 hours of work!

to carry it from the beach to the Annings' house. There it was placed in the Annings' basement—a damp, moldy place that frequently filled with water at high tide. In that miserable room, Mary began to develop her true skill.

The real work of the fossilist isn't the discovery of a fossil, or even the extraction of that fossil from its location. The real work is the cleaning—taking a block of stone and—

Chip-chip-chip-

—slowly, delicately uncovering each individual bone hidden inside. Modern fossil cleaners have the advantage of knowing what they are working on, so they can anticipate where a fin or rib bone will appear in the stone. But Mary was the first person in history to clean a complete skeleton like this. Every time she tapped her hammer, she had no idea what she would find.

The work was tedious, tiring, and dusty. Most days, Mary would only expose an area half the size of a human hand. When the full skeleton was revealed, it was *17 feet long*! It took her almost two years to complete.

It was worth it, though. Mary sold the skeleton for the equivalent of $2,000, the same amount a farmhand would earn in a year. The money helped get the Annings

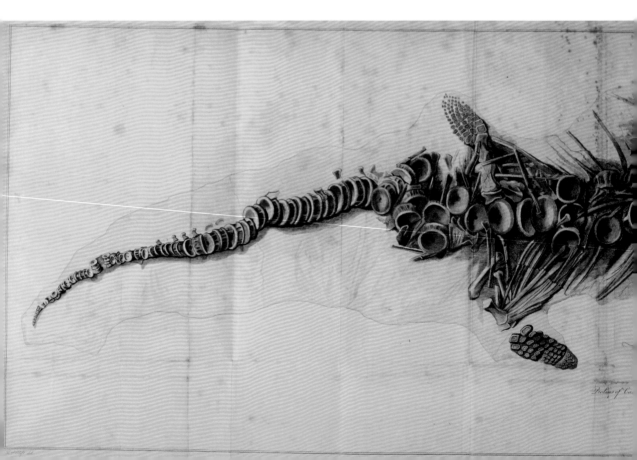

back on their feet. Joseph quit fossiling to get a respectable job making furniture, but Mary had no such choice available to her. In a world where the only possible jobs for a woman were nanny, housemaid, or factory worker, she had found her calling.

Mary became a familiar sight in town. Bundled up against the cold (the best time to hunt for fossils was in the winter after heavy storms had torn open the cliffs), with her rock hammer, her basket, and her dog by her side, Mary was often the only person dedicated enough to explore the dangerous, jagged coastline.

Landslides were frequent. During one particularly large landslide, she came within a few feet of being crushed to death. Her dog wasn't so lucky.

A young lady who sometimes accompanied Mary marveled at Mary's dedication: "We climbed down places, which I would have thought impossible to have descended had I been alone. The wind was high, the ground slippery. . . . In one place she had to make haste to pass between the dashing of two waves. . . ."

Mary Anning's first complete *Ichthyosaurus* (although before it got its proper name, it was named *Proteosaurus*). This illustration, created by the Royal Society, is all that remains of the specimen. The original fossil was destroyed during Nazi bombing of London in World War II.

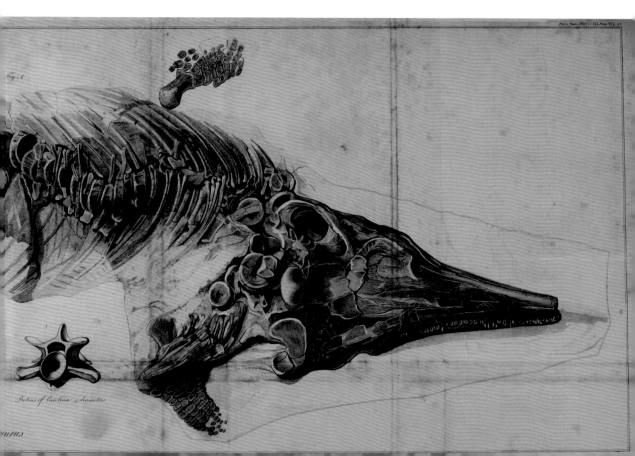

One of only two known images of Mary Anning, 1850. In her hand is a geological hammer. At her feet is her dog, Tray, who died in a landslide that almost claimed Mary's life as well.

And that was just Mary's daily commute.

Only when they arrived at the site did the day's work truly begin—

Chip-chip-chip-

Her work ethic bordered on the superhuman. Mary worked "even when she was so ill that she was brought . . . fainting from the beach." Perhaps this is not so surprising. The gentlemen of Oxford and the Geological Society went fossil hunting for glory. Mary did it to survive.

Fossils were beginning to draw the public's attention. The skull she and her brother found was purchased by a curiosity collector who turned his collection (of 32,000 objects!) into a popular museum. The skull became one of the star attractions. It was unlike any other animal on Earth. For many regular people, it was their first exposure to what geologists had known for 20 years—there were extinct animals in Earth's past.

The Anning skull quickly attracted the attention of the scientific community, too. It had a nose like a dolphin, teeth like a reptile, and when Mary revealed the rest of the body, fins like a fish. In 1821, William Conybeare split the difference by naming it an *Ichthyosaurus* ("fish-lizard").

Like the *Pterodactylus* and the *Mosasaurus*, the *Ichthyosaurus* is not actually a dinosaur. However, this didn't make it any less interesting. What made Mary's discovery unique is that it was a *complete* skeleton.

There was no guessing, no theories about what it might look like, and there was no denying it, either. This was a creature completely foreign to the modern world.

> **"Mary Anning, probably the most important unsung (or inadequately sung) collecting force in the history of paleontology."**
>
> —STEPHEN JAY GOULD,
> HISTORIAN/PALEONTOLOGIST

Geologists became curious about what else could be found in Lyme Regis. William Buckland was one of the first to visit Mary. During his frequent visits to see his aging parents in nearby Axminster, Buckland began spending time with Mary as well. This was highly unusual for the time. One of the great social barriers of nineteenth-century English society was the divide between men and women, but Buckland's enthusiasm for science was so great that he simply didn't care.

Despite spending his childhood around Lyme Regis, Buckland recognized that Mary's knowledge of the cliffs and her fossil-hunting instincts were far superior to his. One visitor marveled that " . . . the moment she finds any bones she knows to what tribe they belong."

With Mary's help, Buckland's fossil collection swelled. His enthusiasm and lack of social graces made his stays at the local hotel legendary. As the other guests at the hotel—well-mannered ladies and gentlemen—tried to eat their breakfast with dignity, Buckland sat in a corner at a breakfast table "loaded with beefsteaks and belemnites . . . toast and trilobites, every table and chair as well as the floor occupied with fossils . . . and heaps of books and papers." Meanwhile, a steady stream of working-class fossil hunters filed into the dining area to "bring their contributions [to Buckland] and receive their pay."

Mary soon received other visitors from the Geological Society. She welcomed the business and attention, but she couldn't help but be curious: *Why* exactly were these gentlemen so interested in fossils?

Like most people at the time, Mary was raised with the idea that Earth was 6,000 years old. She decided to educate herself.

She had help from a childhood friend named Henry Thomas de La Beche. He was a wealthy young man turned geologist who grew up in Lyme Regis and went on fossil hunts with the Annings when they were young. De La Beche and

Buckland freely loaned Mary their books and scientific journals.

Mary built her own reference library by copying their books by hand. She taught herself how to draw by copying the illustrations. She became so good that her work was sometimes indistinguishable from trained artists'. When she learned the importance of Cuvier, she tried to teach herself French so she could correspond with him.

An upper-class woman who was one of Mary's frequent customers marveled at Mary's transformation: "It is certainly a wonderful instance of divine favour—that this poor, ignorant girl should be so blessed, for by reading and application she has arrived to that degree of knowledge as to be in the habit of writing and talking with professors and other clever men on the subject, and they all acknowledge that she understands more of the science than anyone else in this kingdom."

This statement betrays more, perhaps, than its author intended. That a lower-class woman should have enough intelligence to talk to a gentleman must be an act of God. In a society where the upper- and lower-classes rarely mixed, the townspeople were bemused by the

Sir Henry Thomas de La Beche, 1851. Despite his wealthy background, he was a lifelong friend of Mary, and her biggest supporter.

sight of poor Mary and gentlemen like Buckland and de La Beche locked in conversation and hammering rocks side by side.

Chip-chip-chip-

Mary began her fossil-hunting career to earn money, but as she educated herself, she realized there was fame and glory to be had as well. She also knew that she would get none of it.

Between 1815 and 1819, Mary found several more complete skeletons that represented three entirely different species of *Ichthyosaurus*. Conybeare and de La Beche presented these findings to the Geological Society and were showered with praise by their fellow scientists. At no point in their presentation did they mention the name of the young woman who actually found the creatures.

It wasn't personal. Both men were on friendly terms with Anning. It was simply that in the nineteenth century, the scientists, not the fossil collectors, got the credit. And women were not allowed to be scientists. Mary knew very well what their attitude was. Nevertheless, day after day, she picked up her hammer and went back to work. She was about to discover a whole lot more. . . .

Chip-chip-chip-

GIDEON MANTELL

The Annings' first ichthyosaur was more important than anyone realized. It didn't just reveal the existence of a new species. It had become one of the biggest attractions in London. The man who bought the skull remodeled his small museum of curiosities into the Egyptian Hall, a museum in the middle of London that was made to look like an ancient Egyptian temple.

The Egyptian Hall received over 200,000 visitors a year, all of whom filed past the skull in wonder.

It awoke the public to the idea that the

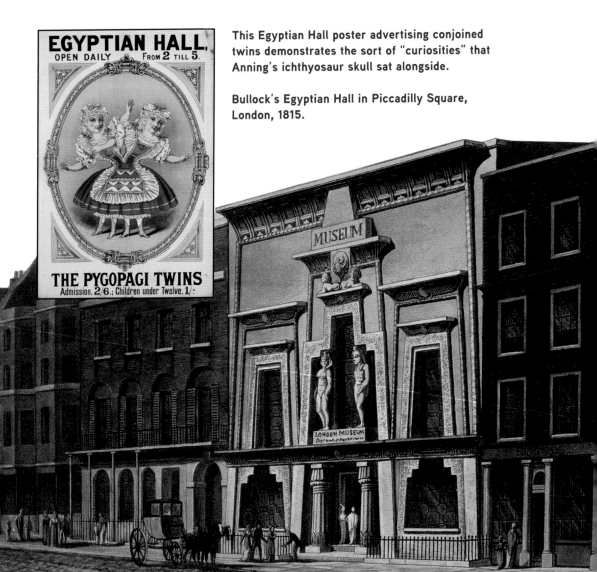

This Egyptian Hall poster advertising conjoined twins demonstrates the sort of "curiosities" that Anning's ichthyosaur skull sat alongside.

Bullock's Egyptian Hall in Piccadilly Square, London, 1815.

Bible's literal truth may not be so literal after all. It also sparked the rational minds of every geologist and fossil hunter in England. The *Ichthyosaurus* was *so* different from our modern world—so flat-out weird—that it encouraged fossil hunters to let their rational minds off the leash and dream about the past. . . .

THE GOOD DOCTOR

Like Mary Anning, Gideon Mantell lived with a powerful sense that he did not belong. The Mantell family had once been aristocrats, knights with money and land. Then in the sixteenth century, one of his ancestors started a rebellion to stop the queen's marriage (religious reasons). The rebellion failed and the queen, somewhat reasonably angry that her wedding had been interrupted, stripped away all of the Mantells' wealth. By the time Gideon was born, in 1790, his family had been reduced to simple shoemakers in a country village called Lewes, which was close to Lyme Regis's Jurassic Coast.

At an early age, it was obvious that Gideon was a gifted child. He was able to recite the Bible by heart. Unfortunately, his family was Methodist, and the state religion of England was Anglican. This meant that Mantell was barred from attending grammar schools and universities.

Mantell was homeschooled and eventually went to the fantastically named alternative academy, the Dissenting School for Boys. His family then sent him to London to train as a doctor. It was the best job available to someone of his intelligence without a university degree.

Once he got his medical license, he returned to the quiet of Lewes (too quiet, it must have seemed, after the buzz of London) and took up the life of a country doctor. He settled down, married the daughter of one of his patients,

Dr. Gideon Mantell, 1837.

After he studied medicine in London, the local hospital in Lewes must have been a letdown for Mantell.

and became a respectable member of the community.

Financially, the job was rewarding. Someone willing to work hard could make good money, and Mantell's work ethic was legendary. Using only a saw, a scalpel, and a jar of leeches, Mantell dealt with every form of medical emergency. He delivered 200 to 300 babies a year(!), pulled teeth, amputated limbs, and worst of all, treated the injuries of young children who worked in the mills among the giant, crushing gears. Many of those younger patients didn't survive,

but Mantell had no time to mourn.

He was the only doctor within miles, so no matter what happened to his patient, he had to get on his horse and ride to the next town, to the next patient. Mantell saw between 40 and 50 patients *a day*. He only slept four hours a night, or sometimes not at all. During an outbreak of the plague, he treated patients for *six days straight* without sleep.

With this grinding schedule, his rides from one town to the next were often his only downtime. But instead of resting, that's when Mantell took the opportunity to indulge his true passion. You see, ever since he was a teenager, Gideon Mantell had led a double life.

This was Mantell's view as he rode from village to village making doctor's visits. But in his sketch pad, he recorded what he thought lay underneath. In the strata beneath these hills lay two of his most famous dinosaur discoveries.

THE SECRET FOSSILIST

Gideon Mantell did not want to be a humble country doctor. He wanted fame, awards, recognition. He wanted to escape the tedium of his country-bumpkin town and move to the big cities where his brilliance would be recognized and he would be admitted into prestigious scientific societies.

> ## "Unravel the mysteries of this beautiful world . . ."
>
> —GIDEON MANTELL,
> ON THE PURPOSE OF SCIENCE

Gideon Mantell wanted to be a geologist. A famous fossil hunter. A scientist.

In nineteenth-century England, fossils were a regular part of life for any child who grew up in the countryside. But Mantell never grew out of his fascination with their strangeness. When he left home to get his medical degree, he brought a bag of his favorite fossils with him.

Mantell arrived in London as an impressionable, fossil-loving teenager just when the ideas of geology were beginning to bubble up into popular culture. The Geological Society had just been founded. Bookshops displayed books with intriguing titles like *Memoirs of Mammoth, and Various Other Extraordinary and Stupendous Bones.* That was the first book Mantell bought for himself in London.

The second book he purchased was his favorite, *Organic Remains of a Former World*, by Dr. James Parkinson. Dr. Parkinson was one of the founders of the Geological Society, but more importantly he lived in London. One day, Mantell gathered up all of his fan-

Blue Marl. Green Sand. Oak Tree Clay. with Beds of Limestone &c. Ferruginous Sand. Formation. Crowborough Beacon 804 Ft. North

the South Eastern part of Sussex.

boy courage and knocked on Parkinson's door. To his delight, Parkinson answered . . . and invited him in.

Over cups of tea, Dr. Parkinson filled Mantell's head with the ideas of Cuvier and "former worlds." Parkinson was especially devoted to William Smith's study of strata. After that meeting, Mantell dutifully returned to his medical training, but he had bigger plans in mind.

He would become the doctor his family wanted him to be, but in his free time, he would map the strata of his hometown. And that was just the beginning. Mapping strata meant hunting for fossils. Fossil hunting meant he might discover something new.

The year that he moved back to Lewes, Mary Anning's *Ichthyosaurus* appeared at the Egyptian Hall, capturing the attention of London. Perhaps, thought Mantell, he too could capture the attention of the biggest city in the world. Perhaps he might find a monster from a former world buried in his own backyard.

It turned out, he was wrong. There wasn't one.

There were two.

OBSESSION

The main road that passes through Lewes was a popular route for tourists traveling to seaside resort towns like Lyme Regis. Maintaining the roads required gravel, so rock quarries appeared all over the county,

carving into the hills. It was a geologist's dream, and on his rides from patient to patient, Mantell stopped at every one.

The quarry workers knew the hills better than anyone, so Mantell talked to them daily. He paid them to deliver every specimen they found to his house, much to the dismay of his wife, Mary. He soon filled the entire first floor of their home with fossils, forcing the family to live up on the second floor.

This was an expensive habit. Though Mantell earned a good living as a doctor, his fossil obsession kept his family in financial trouble his entire life. When poverty eventually forced him to sell his collection, it contained 20,000 fossils.

Money wasn't the only thing Mantell sacrificed. Each person in this book had a very specific job that he or she did well— William Smith mapped strata, Mary Anning found and cleaned fossils, William Buckland and Conybeare examined and assembled fossils, and Cuvier identified them.

Gideon Mantell, on the other hand, did it all. He had to. He was an amateur working on his own. To accomplish all of this required time. Time and obsession. He worked late every night—chiseling, cleaning, cataloguing, writing, and illustrating. He pushed his body and mind to their limits. He sacrificed sleep, his social life, even his health.

Mantell suffered from scoliosis, a

In this illustration by Gideon's wife, Mary, we see that Gideon's fossil-hunting obsession extended into their family time during the weekends. He took his wife and children with him to the quarries. In a sign of things to come, Mary pictures herself and her child on the left, backs turned and walking away, while Gideon, hammer in hand, is too busy to notice.

condition where the spine grows in a curve. Bending over his workbench night after night for hours on end was agonizing, but he pushed through the pain because he was fixated on the pursuit of knowledge . . . and glory.

The work began to pay off. A picture of the former world beneath his home county of Sussex slowly came into focus. The Geological Society's maps indi-cated that the local strata had been formed by an ocean, like Lyme Regis. But Mantell was finding tree leaves, plant stems, and even a fossilized palm tree.

The society's maps, he realized, were wrong. This area had once been dry land.

Mantell started to realize that he had a true talent for this. He was making dis-coveries that contradicted the experts in the field. He decided to advertise his abil-ities by self-publishing a massive book titled *The Fossils of the South Downs*. It was going to be a complete geolog-ical and fossil survey of his home county. His wife, Mary, taught herself anatomi-cal illustration to help his efforts.

Fossilized ferns like this helped convince Mantell that in the geological past the South Downs had been dry land.

The only limit to Mantell's ambitions was time. Between the research, writing, and the fact that he already had a full-time job, the book took him four years to complete. For four years, Mantell reconstructed the lost world of Sussex by combing through thousands of fossils and rocks that arrived in a steady stream at his front door, sent to him by the local quarrymen.

If there were any monsters buried beneath the town, between the ceaseless efforts of the quarrymen and Mantell, it was only a matter of time before they found them.

THE QUARRYMEN

Let us pause for a moment and think about death.

When a sea creature dies, it sinks gently to the bottom of the sea. Scavengers and invertebrates like worms clean the flesh off its bones. Then, silt rains down on it; sand gently piles over it. This layer of mud condenses into a strata, freezing those bones in place. So when someone like Mary Anning discovers it 200 million years later, there's

Photo of Stonesfield slate miners taken in 1905. Since slate mining was a family business, some of these men would have been the grandchildren of the miners who found the original *Megalosaurus* bones.

a good chance of finding the entire skeleton perfectly preserved in the rock.

Mary Anning's discoveries (and Cuvier's *Mosasaurus*) were sea creatures. They were not dinosaurs, even though they lived at the same time. Dinosaurs are a class of reptiles that mostly lived on land. This made it far more difficult to discover them. When a land creature dies, its body suffers a much harsher fate.

Scavengers tear at it. Bones scatter as animals drag their chunk of the body back to their lair. Someone exploring the death scene 200 million years later will only find individual bones scattered across a wide area . . . a leg bone over here, a broken rib over there.

David Oliver, Charles Howes, John Oliver—these are not famous names. You won't find them in any books on the history of paleontology, but they are just as important as Cuvier and Buckland.

David Oliver
found a large Ribb Boone
abought too feet in Length
But very mutch Broken
Sir, if you pleas to come an See them.

December 3, 1814
Ther is a Large Boone found in a
Sleat Pit very perfect not Broken

in a Large Stone the property of
Charles Howes, Sleate Digger.

John Oliver have Leatly found a
Large Boone very mutch Broken
suposed to be Some part of a Horse.

These are some of the semiliterate, anonymous men who worked by candlelight in the dark underground quarries of Stonesfield. These were the men who dug up the bones of *Megalosaurus*. It was the uneducated laborers like these who were responsible for most of the discoveries around Europe at the time. To recognize and retrieve one whole skeleton the way Mary Anning did is a remarkable achievement. To recognize and retrieve enough scattered bones (some of them barely visible inside a block of stone) to form a skeleton is impossible without the help of an army.

What did Buckland's hometown of Axminster and Mantell's Lewes have in common? Gravel roads.

Why did Oxford produce so many fossils? It needed stone for its buildings.

What made it possible for Smith to analyze the geological formation of the planet? Canals.

If you had to point to one thing and say that it was responsible for the discovery of dinosaurs and our understanding of the planet, it would be . . . infrastructure.

During the Industrial Revolution, workers burrowed underground for coal, carved into land to build canals, railroads, and gravel roads. Their days were full of exhausting physical labor, but they quickly learned to spot even the smallest of fossils in the rock. Around the town of Lewes, every quarry worker knew he could earn extra money by sending fossils to Gideon Mantell. In the village of Stonesfield, outside Oxford, the houses became "a succession of fossil shops containing specimens."

The Stonesfield slate diggers developed a keen eye for fossils in the razor-thin slate sheets they were pulling from the quarry. They each kept a personal stash of small fossils to sell to curious tourists. But they knew to reserve the really spectacular finds for "the college folk" like William Buckland.

They didn't really understand why Buckland was so interested in these bones, but they were more than happy to be his scouts. As the head of the Ashmolean, Buckland used the museum's funds to buy one fossil for the equivalent of $53,000!

William Buckland largely ignored the rigid class barriers in English society that separated the rich from the poor. He recognized that the quarry workers had a lot to teach any scientist who would listen. In fact, he spent so much time in quarries that whenever someone else took his horse for a ride, the horse would stop at every single quarry and refuse to move until the rider dismounted and pretended to look at rocks for a while.

Since fossils are usually embedded inside rock, they need to be cleaned with a hammer and chisel to reveal the contours within. It's an art form, requiring patience and the precision of a sculptor. Paleontology is a science of very minor details. Every minor crack or curve in a bone can tell an entire story about that animal. Mary Anning mastered this skill, but so did many of the quarry workers as well.

The gentlemen of the scientific societies and museums soon learned that if they wanted a fossil cleaned properly, they needed to hire a quarry worker. These men quite literally had the best hands-on knowledge of stone in the country. So in the back rooms of museums, anonymous men cleaned the fossils that would make history.

THE FINAL BONES

Buckland continued to visit the Stonesfield quarries. In the few years that he lived at the Ashmolean, the number of dinosaur bones in the collection swelled from two or three to fifteen.

There were limb bones. Bits of rib and hip.

Buckland had finally assembled all of the pieces of *Megalosaurus* together.

Finally, there was enough for someone to recognize that a brand-new species had appeared. But it wouldn't be Buckland. His specialty was geology, rocks, and minerals. Analyzing these bones required someone who specialized in anatomy.

It required the great Cuvier.

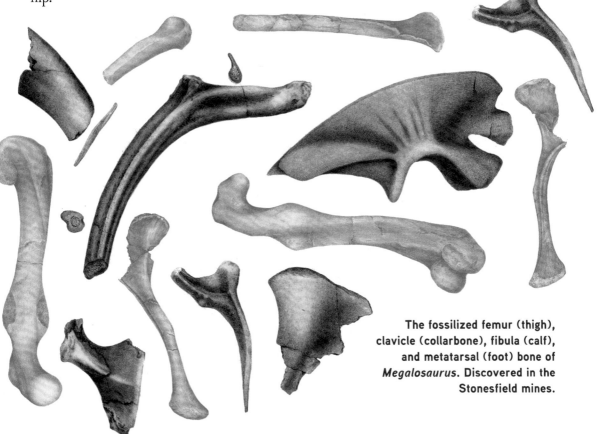

The fossilized femur (thigh),
clavicle (collarbone), fibula (calf),
and metatarsal (foot) bone of
Megalosaurus. Discovered in the
Stonesfield mines.

THE ELEPHANT MAN AT THE ASHMOLEAN

Science is based on information. The faster that information flows between scientists, the faster discoveries can be made. Unfortunately, between 1803 and 1815, the flow of information between France and England stopped.

The two countries were at war, and the British navy set up a blockade across the English Channel. The same wars that forced English tourists to visit Mary Anning in Lyme Regis also prevented the French from coming to England.

Cuvier's books and ideas on extinction made it to England before the blockade, sparking a surge in fossil hunting. Because of its unique geology, England was a rich source of fossils. But when it came time to analyze those fossils, Cuvier was stuck on the other side of the channel. Scientific progress slowed down for years while the war dragged on.

When the war finally ended in 1815, information once again flowed freely between the countries. Letters from Buckland and Conybeare informed Cuvier of all the discoveries the English had made during the war. Cuvier was constantly searching for more extinct animals to identify, so in 1818, he visited England to see their fossils for himself.

Cuvier's trip centered around two

For any dinosaur lover, this is one of the high points in the history of paleontology—the meeting of the leader of English geology and the leader of French paleontology. This is the moment that humans looked into the past and saw a dinosaur staring back at them.

main destinations—the huge fossil collection that later became the Natural History Museum in London, and the Ashmolean collection in Oxford. To say that Buckland was excited is an understatement. Cuvier was his hero.

Buckland personally guided Cuvier through the vast Ashmolean collection—the combined efforts of the Tradescants, Elias Ashmole, the learned Dr. Plot, and every other keeper that had come before him. As he did, he must have wondered what would catch Cuvier's eye.

Cuvier zeroed in on the pile of fifteen bones from the Stonesfield quarry—Sir Pegge's jawbone, Webb's vertebrae, and the bits and pieces assembled by Buckland.

It's a confusing specimen. These fossils were (and still are) an incomplete record. None of the bones are from the same individual. Some are from juveniles, some from adults. This accounted for some of Buckland's hesitation in analyzing them. But Cuvier had no problem. Using the same methods he had applied to the mastodon, the key for Cuvier was the teeth. He observed:

■ All of the teeth in the jaw were the same shape. There were no grinding molars. This is typical of a reptile.

■ Small replacement teeth were growing next to the adult teeth. This is another trait typical of a reptile.

■ A crocodile's jaw is long and thin, but this lower jaw was short, narrow, and flat. This was similar to a monitor lizard.

No record exists of the conversation between Cuvier and Buckland, but after Cuvier left England, he wrote: "At Oxford, I saw a much larger species . . . entirely like a crocodile, but of a length more than three times that of our crocodiles of 15 and 18 feet, [it] announced a truly gigantic animal."

Buckland, as usual, was a bit more expressive: "Cuvier has no doubt that the great Stonesfield beast was a monitor [lizard] 40 feet long and as big as an elephant."

Cuvier had already identified reptiles like the *Mosasaurus*, but those were sea creatures. This creature from Stonesfield, however, was a land lizard unlike anything living today.

Cuvier had, in fact, identified the first dinosaur.

But . . . the bones were from England. They had been gathered by Englishmen. Cuvier knew that it was not his place to announce this discovery. That honor would fall to Buckland, but incredibly, it took until 1824—*another six years!*—before Buckland presented this breakthrough to his fellow scientists.

The question, of course, is why.

● ●

THE DIPLOMAT

Neil deGrasse Tyson. Carl Sagan. William Buckland was one of the first in a long line of educators whose mission was to bring science to the masses. Buckland sometimes spoke to crowds of a thousand, trying to convince the highly religious public that they had nothing to fear from the discoveries of science. He was not always successful.

Why did it take six years for William Buckland to announce the somewhat amazing discovery of a 40-foot land reptile, an entirely new form of creature?

There are many theories:

Perhaps he was afraid of stepping on the wrong toes. Buckland's salary was paid by the Church of England. When he was made professor of geology, he gave a speech in which he promised that his new science of geology would act as a "handmaiden" to God. It would advance our understanding of the Bible by proving that God's "works" (Earth) and His "words" (the Bible) were one and the same. Nowhere in the Bible was there a mention of 40-foot reptiles as big as elephants.

Perhaps Buckland simply didn't know that they had uncovered anything exceptional. At that time, almost every fossil that came out of the ground was a mind-blowing discovery: Flying Reptiles! Giant Sloths!

Reptile Fish! When every bone belongs to some never-before-imagined creature, it is hard to know what to prioritize.

Perhaps he was waiting to collect more bones to make the skeleton complete. Fifteen bones may have been enough for the famous Cuvier to work with, but it was not enough to truly convince the outside world. Buckland was very wary of being wrong. Every geologist knew the story of Beringer's Lying Stones.

In eighteenth-century Germany, a group of students decided to play a prank on a professor they hated named Johann Beringer. They carved stones into fake fossils and planted them in locations where they knew he went fossiling. Beringer discovered them and excitedly published his findings. When it was revealed that he had been duped, he spent his own money trying to buy back all his books to prevent disgrace, after which he sued the pants off the two students and everyone wound up poor, miserable, and in court. Perhaps Buckland was wise to be somewhat cautious.

All of these theories are probably a little bit correct, but the simplest explanation is perhaps the most accurate one. William Buckland was a very, very busy man.

By making himself the best-known fossilist in England, Buckland became the focal point of fossil research for the entire British Empire. Reports of fossils poured in from all over the planet—a Jamaican woolly mammoth, a Siberian rhinoceros, fossilized ferns from the desert of Libya.

It was impossible not to be swept up in the pace of discovery, although Buckland did manage to keep a cool head. When informed by a breathless correspondent in South America that explorers had uncovered evidence of a unicorn, Buckland wrote back that it was "probably a red deer that had lost a horn."

Besides processing all of this information, Buckland lectured and kept up his own fieldwork. Along the way, he expanded our vision of the past from a few extinct animals to an entire Lost World.

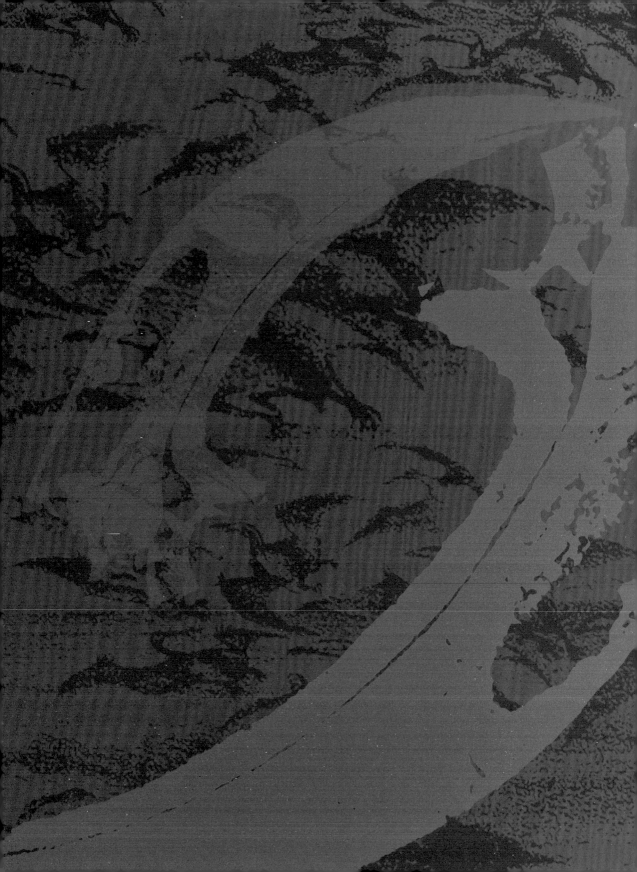

WILLIAM, BILLY, AND THE CAVE OF BONES

William Buckland was on his hands and knees, crawling deeper and deeper into a cave . . .

25 feet . . .

50 feet . . .

. . . and the daylight began to fade. Buckland paused long enough to light a candle; then he kept going. He believed he was about to make the great breakthrough of his career.

From the moment he became Oxford's professor of geology, he'd dedicated himself to finding proof that the Bible was true. William Buckland was stuck between two eras. He was the most enthusiastic cheerleader for science of his time, but he was also the son of a reverend. He had

struggled to reconcile his faith in both. But inside this cave, he believed, was the evidence he needed.

So he crawled deeper . . . 100 feet . . . 200 feet . . .

. . . then the tunnel opened up into a large cave and, in the light of his candle, Buckland saw the bones.

Hundreds of them. Bones of every shape and size jumbled together. Some trapped in stalagmites growing up from the floor. Some sticking out of mud on the floor "like the legs of pigeon through a pie-crust." All of them were cracked and broken by some mysterious force.

The entrance to the Kirkdale Cave had been found by quarry workers, of course. They didn't go inside, though. They just scooped up some gravel and bones near the entrance to pour onto a local road.

A local doctor strolling down the road contacted Buckland, because these were no ordinary bones.

They looked like hyena bones. There was one rather large problem with that—

Hyenas don't live in England.

Buckland immediately went to investigate. To him, the explanation seemed obvious. Surely, the biblical flood had swept up enormous herds of animals from Africa and carried them halfway around the world into the hills of northern England. In one fell swoop, this would prove the deluge (and therefore, the Bible) was true *and* explain how Cuvier's extinct species went extinct.

> "The great tragedy of science—the slaying of a beautiful hypothesis by an ugly fact."
>
> —ALDOUS HUXLEY

The cave was a perfectly preserved time capsule of the past. Nothing in it had ever been seen or touched by a human being. All Buckland had to do was read the bones and the past would be revealed.

Wearing a top hat and academic robe

William Buckland among his many specimens.

(his typical field outfit), Buckland carefully catalogued every single bone. But the more he worked, the more confused he became. Nothing in the cave fit into his flood theory.

THE CAVE OF MYSTERY

Here were Buckland's problems:

- There weren't just hyena bones in the Kirkdale Cave. There were bones of elephants, mammoths, hippos, rhinos, and more. But to get into the cave, Buckland had been forced to crawl on his hands and

knees. How could a fully grown elephant or hippo fit through that entrance?

- He noticed that "every bone had marks on it that indicated it had been chewed. . . ." Suppose for a moment that a flood *had* somehow squeezed an elephant down a narrow 200-foot tunnel. Why, then, would a gigantic mass of swirling water only leave behind bones that were chewed?

- The bones represented 24 different species, but there were 75 individual hyena skeletons, far outnumbering the other species. Wouldn't a massive flood have left behind a more random selection of bones?

- Scattered around the cave were hundreds of small hard white balls (pictured, bottom right). What the heck were those?

He was faced with a seemingly unsolvable riddle. Fortunately, there has never been a greater match of an investigator's professional and personal interest. The clue to unlocking the mystery of the Kirkdale Cave lay in Buckland's greatest passion—food.

THE STOMACH RULES THE WORLD

No one knows quite why William Buckland ate what he did: poverty, publicity, curiosity, or biblical inspiration (Genesis 9:3: "Every moving thing that liveth shall be meat for you . . ."). Maybe he just got hungry while he spent so much time working in caves.

Whatever the reason, Buckland ate every animal he could find—panthers, porpoises, roasted hedgehogs, rhino pie, ostrich, bear, elephant trunks, and kangaroo. For breakfast, he served crocodile steak. At parties, batter-fried mouse on toast. Family dinners involved horse parts and insects of every kind.

Eating at this level was more than just a hobby or sport. It was Buckland's guiding philosophy. In the classroom, he would race up to his students, slashing a fossilized jaw at their faces, and scream, "WHAT RULES THE WORLD?!"

He then calmly informed the terrified students, "The stomach, sir, rules the world. The great ones eat the less, the less the lesser still."

With that in mind, Buckland noticed

THE BUCKLAND FAMILY ZOO

Alongside Tiglath the bear, William Buckland's home was filled with animals. The dining room was stacked with cages of snakes, frogs, and turtles. His living room was home to a monkey and free-roaming guinea pigs . . . until one party when a student noted, "I took care to tuck up my legs on the sofa, for fear of a casual bite from a jackal that was wandering around the room. After a while I heard the animal munching up something under the sofa . . . I told Buckland. 'My poor guinea pigs!' he exclaimed, and sure enough, four of the five of them had perished."

that the deep grooves on the cracked edges of the bones closely matched the hyena teeth in the cave. Since all of the bones exhibited the same bite patterns, then perhaps there was an alternate explanation to the flood. Perhaps the Kirkdale Cave was a hyena den.

Hyenas are scavengers, so they wouldn't pull an entire elephant through the narrow cave entrance. They would only drag in one limb at a time. Everything about his new theory made perfect sense. Now he had to prove it.

Cuvier's biggest breakthrough came by comparing an extinct elephant to a modern elephant, so Buckland decided to do the same. He needed to examine a hyena skull and its teeth.

He contacted the owner of a London menagerie (a type of early zoo) who owned a hyena. The owner was too fond of his hyena (he'd named him Billy) to turn him into a skull, but he offered Buckland an alternative: take Billy for a little while as a pet.

For most people, the idea of making a hyena a house pet would be a bit daunting. The hyena is one of the most feared animals in Africa, and with good reason. Its jaws are among the most powerful in nature. But William Buckland was not most people. Alongside all of his other extraordinary habits, he had turned his home into a minor zoo.

Buckland took Billy in and put him to work.

BILLY CRACKS THE CASE

Buckland presented Billy with the shinbone of an ox. Watching Billy eat reminded Buckland of watching "a miner's crushing mill." He rejoiced in a letter to a friend that when Billy finished, he left behind "precisely those parts which are left at Kirkdale. . . . So wonderfully alike were these bones in their fracture . . . that it is impossible to say which bone had been cracked by Billy and which by the hyenas of Kirkdale!"

Having a live hyena provided Buckland with more proof than he had counted on. The small white balls that were scattered around the cave had mystified Buckland, but the menagerie keeper immediately recognized them as the sort of feces produced by the bone-heavy diet of a hyena.

This caught Buckland's attention. He was fascinated with what he called "coprolites" but we would call feces, solid waste or, more plainly, poo.

Buckland realized that if Billy's postmeal poo matched the balls in the cave, it was further proof that ancient hyenas not only ate in the cave, but lived there as well.

So Buckland waited. And later that evening . . . "as the ancient beasts deposited [bone-filled feces] in abundance after a dinner of bones, so did [Billy] deposit

pounds of the same substance."

The proof was in the pooing.

MR. BUCKLAND PRESENTS . . .

In 1822, Buckland presented to the Royal Society the most detailed picture of ancient England ever seen.

Kirkdale had been a hyena paradise. Below the cave was a lake that the hyenas had used as a personal snack bar. They scavenged whatever they could find from the lake—from rhinos to rats—and dragged it back to their lair to eat in peace.

In this one lecture, Buckland invented an entirely new field of science—it came to be known as

IN PRAISE OF POO

Despite his quirks, William Buckland was not a nut job. Fossilized poo is a paleontologist's best friend. Coprolites are a record of what an animal eats. They provide a snapshot of the plants and animals that existed at the same time.

Of course, not everyone understood this, and Buckland's enthusiasm became a source of worry. One friend warned him that he was in serious danger of getting "the reputation of too frequently and too minutely examining faecal products."

Buckland, as usual, took this as encouragement to be even more outrageous. He built an entire coffee table out of fossilized feces (see above). One of his favorite party tricks was to serve food to guests on that table. Then, halfway through the meal, he would inform them what the table was made from.

• •

paleoecology, the study of ecosystems of the past and how ancient animals interacted with their environment. Now we didn't just see an extinct animal, we saw the Lost World it lived in.

But when he published his findings in a book in 1823, Buckland showed that the two central ideas in his life—science and religeon—were increasingly coming into conflict.

Religious Buckland claimed that the Kirkdale Cave actually *proved* the biblical flood was real. The total *lack* of hyenas now living in Kirkdale, he claimed, proved that they had run away to avoid something. It must have been the flood.

However, he also seemed to be pull-ing away from the traditional views of his biblical upbringing. Buckland estimated that the hyena den was *at least* 5,000 to 6,000 years old (modern carbon dating has shown that it was, in fact, almost 120,000 years old). He also admitted that the deluge wasn't responsible for floating herds of animals around the world. It was only responsible for the thin layer of mud in the cave.

The fundamentalist religious community was enraged. "The result of the most inconsiderate ignorance!" stormed one theologian. Buckland was "ungodly," an "infidel philosopher" who tried to "distort every fact of science . . . against the Scriptures of eternal truth."

Despite the criticism, the book sold out

❧ BUCKLAND BACK IN TIME ❧

William Conybeare couldn't resist poking a little fun at his old road-trip buddy. After Buckland's speech at the Geological Society, Conybeare passed around a picture he drew of Buckland encountering the hyenas in their den. It was done in jest, but without knowing it, Conybeare created a little piece of history.

This is the first image of mankind interacting with the prehistoric past. Conybeare turned Buckland into one of the first time travelers ever pictured.

immediately. Thanks to Buckland and Billy, more people were beginning to understand what geologists now accepted as fact. In the gaps of the Bible's story, there was enough time for England to be a tropical island (!) teeming with hyenas and elephants.

There was even enough time to imagine something far stranger, something not even mentioned in the Bible, like giant reptiles.

And it was possible to discover all of this, Buckland showed, through the intense study of something as small as the marks made by a tooth.

"EXTRAORDINARY AND STUPENDOUS BONES"

The village of Lewes is a small, quiet place. If you rode through it late at night, every house would be dark . . . except one. There was always a candle burning in the first-floor window of the local doctor, Gideon Mantell. This was his workshop, where he worked on his fossil collection every night into the early hours of the morning.

If you peered through his front window in 1821, you would see him bent over his workbench, all of his immense concentration focused on a tooth.

It was the tooth of a carnivore—three inches long, sharp, and serrated like a steak knife. It had arrived from the quarrymen along with a broken femur—just a *piece* of femur, mind you—that was 2.5 feet long and 25 inches around!

Mantell was almost finished writing his book *The Fossils of the South Downs*. He'd filled it with his wife's precise illustrations of leaves, shells, and other small specimens. But this tooth and femur practically merited an entire book themselves. These were some of the "extraordinary and stupendous bones" he'd read about as a young man.

> ## "I think you will accuse me of indulging in the marvelous. . . ."
> —GIDEON MANTELL

They were found inside strata that we now know as the Cretaceous Period (about 145 to 65 million years ago). Modern paleontologists know that some small mammals existed during that time, but when Mantell was working, the Cretaceous was considered part of Cuvier's "Age of Reptiles." As far as Mantell knew, no mammals existed back then.

This could only mean one thing. . . .

Mantell's "Tooth of an animal of the Lizard Tribe."

Mantell concluded that giant land-dwelling reptiles once roamed Earth.

It was an extraordinary leap of imagination, but what made it even more impressive was the fact that Mantell made it all on his own, using only the fossils from his hometown and his deductive reasoning.

Mantell was very confident in his abilities, but still, the situation seemed strange to him. Was he really the *only* one who had discovered this? He was an amateur. Why hadn't he heard this idea from any professional scientists?

Because Buckland hadn't published anything about his meeting with Cuvier, Mantell had no idea that in the Ashmolean Museum there was a pile of bones from the Stonesfield quarries that would confirm his theory.

At least he didn't . . . until there was a knock on his front door.

GEOLOGY KNOCKS

When Mantell opened the door, he found himself facing a young man named Charles Lyell who would change his life.

Years later, Charles Lyell would become the most influential geologist in history. He popularized the ideas that form modern geology. He influenced Charles Darwin and the theory of evolution. But before all of that, he entered Oxford University with the intention of being a lawyer. That is, until he took a

class taught by the charismatic Professor William Buckland.

Buckland was so captivating that the young Lyell, like Mantell, developed a double life. His profession was the law, but his passion was geology. Whenever he traveled, he liked to search the local quarries for fossils. By sheer coincidence, he went on holiday near Lewes, but at every quarry he visited he heard the same refrain—there were no fossils for sale. They'd all been purchased by the local doctor. This roused Lyell's curiosity, so he

Charles Lyell—geologist, Buckland's pupil, and Mantell's soon-to-be savior.

found the home of Gideon Mantell and knocked on the door.

Mantell was honored to meet Lyell. He craved attention from the scientific community. Lyell wasn't a world famous geologist yet, but he was an Oxford man and a student of Buckland. Lyell spent two days poring over Mantell's collection. Eventually, Mantell worked up the nerve to show Lyell his most closely guarded treasure—the monstrous tooth and bones from his "land reptile."

To Mantell's amazement, Lyell didn't bat an eye. Mantell's fossils were identical to Buckland's *Megalosaurus* bones. So Lyell told him the most important news of all—the great Cuvier himself had confirmed the idea that there must have been an ancient species of giant land reptiles.

Mantell was overjoyed. He wasn't crazy!

The most important geologists in England and France had confirmed his theory. This gave Mantell the boost he needed to finish his book. He didn't try to claim the discovery of the carnivore reptile as his own, though. He knew Buckland had beaten him to it.

Buckland had more bones, Cuvier's blessing, and a famous name. More importantly, Buckland could get his discovery published in the Geological Society's journal far faster than a nobody like Mantell. Buckland's delay, however, did mean that Mantell's book created its own piece of history. When he published *The Fossils of the South Downs* in 1822, he wrote about the creatures he was sure were buried underneath his local hills:

> "There are one or more gigantic animals of the Lizard Tribe."

The word "dinosaur" wouldn't be invented until 1842, but this was the very first reference in print to the existence of dinosaurs.

Despite being competitive and desperate for attention, Mantell didn't mind too much that he'd missed out on claiming credit for this discovery. That's because some time in 1822, he received another incredible stroke of luck. He found another tooth.

But this tooth was different. Very different.

THE TOOTH WHISPERER

In 1822, we would find Mantell in almost exactly the same pose as he had been the year before. Bent over his workbench late at night, staring at a tooth. The fact is, Mantell barely left his study except to see patients. He resented the nights that his wife invited friends over for dinner.

Mantell didn't need friends. He had fossils. And this particular fossil was absolutely riveting.

It wasn't as dramatic as the carnivorous tooth. It was less than an inch wide.

There are several stories about how the tooth came to him. Some claim his wife, Mary, found it on a gravel road as she waited for him to see a patient. Others claim, less dramatically, that he simply received it from one of the many quarrymen he befriended.

Mantell didn't have enough time to analyze this new tooth properly for his book, so he simply listed it as "Teeth and Bones of Unknown Animal." But the more he studied it, the more he believed this "unknown animal" was the answer to all his prayers.

Cuvier and Buckland had both shown the importance of teeth to paleontology.

A single tooth can tell an entire story—an animal's age (how worn is it?), the world it lived in and its diet (sharp teeth for meat, molars for plants), its body structure (predators and prey are built very differently), and its size.

Over the course of many nights, Mantell studied this tooth, trying to understand the story it had to tell. His problem was its story sounded too incredible to be true:

■ It was a molar, flat and worn down on top from grinding food. It was very obviously the tooth of an herbivorous (plant-eating) animal.

■ It was .8 inches wide but 2.83 inches tall. That is not quite as large as the 3-inch

The tooth hidden in the gravel of a country road. Possibly found by Mary Mantell.

Gideon's long-suffering wife, Mary Mantell.

carnivore teeth of *Megalosaurus*, but it implied that the creature was almost as big as an elephant.

■ Because of the palm trees and leaves in the same strata, it had to be a land animal.

■ The small indents at the bottom of the tooth made room for replacement teeth to grow. This is a typical reptile trait.

> "When you have eliminated the impossible, whatever remains, however improbable, must be the truth."
>
> —SHERLOCK HOLMES

This was Mantell's improbable truth—there once lived an herbivorous, land-dwelling reptile that was as large as an elephant. The "improbable" part was that, as far as Mantell knew, *there was no such thing as a plant-eating reptile!* The only reptiles he had ever heard of ate meat.

Mantell had a dilemma. If he could convince others that he was right (and he was *sure* he was right), he would be famous. But who would listen to him?

His story didn't make any sense.

THE TRAVELS OF THE TOOTH
PART 1: LONDON
JUNE 1822

Gideon Mantell stepped into a carriage with his bag held tightly in his hands. Inside weren't his usual knives and jars of leeches. Today, his bag contained all of his hopes and dreams . . . and the tooth.

A groundbreaking scientific discovery is no good if it's all in your head. He had to convince the scientific community that he was right. But he had no connections. Because of his religion, he hadn't gone to the right schools. Because of his family, he lived in the country. He was a nobody.

He tried inviting William Buckland to see his collection: "I have been anxiously expecting the pleasure of a visit from you, but begin to despair. . . ." Since Buckland was too busy to visit him, Mantell decided to make the first move. The Geological Society was meeting in London, and Mantell was determined be there.

Traveling to London back then wasn't easy. It took hours, and required many stops to change horses. The carriage wheels on gravel roads made it a bone-rattling, physically exhausting experience, but Mantell didn't mind. The only thing he couldn't endure was being ignored.

He had pinned all his hopes on the publication of his book, and at first, things looked promising. The king of England himself had purchased a copy for his library. The king! This made Mantell

"I am resolved to make every possible effort
to obtain that rank in society to which I
feel I am entitled both by my education and
my profession."

—GIDEON MANTELL'S JOURNAL, MAY 1822

so sure his book would be a hit with the upper-class scientific community that he set the book's price at $1,000 per copy.

The book flopped.

To cover his losses, Mantell had to borrow money from his wife's brother. This wasn't the last time he would borrow money from his wife's family to fuel his fossil habit. Mantell abandoned the idea of publishing his way into scientific stardom. He needed to make his case in person.

The carriage drove straight to the heart of London. Mantell stepped out onto a street bursting with noise—pubs, theaters, street merchants shouting their prices, ladies selling flowers, and more. He wasn't in the country anymore. This was 20 Bedford Street, the House of the Geological Society. This, Mantell thought, was where he belonged.

The Geological Society began as a chummy gentlemen's club for men to eat, drink, and be merry while talking rocks. By the 1820s, geology had become a more serious profession. Trained scientists like Buckland had taken charge . . . but it was still a gentlemen's club. They lectured and argued about science, but they also socialized, drank wine, and burst into group sing-alongs of geology-themed songs.

Into this walked Gideon Mantell—an intense, desperate, sleep-deprived outsider. He wasn't from Oxford or Cambridge. He wasn't aristocratic or rich. He wasn't a professor, or even an engineer. He was just a dude who really, really loved fossils.

You can imagine the members' reactions when he passed around a pretty ordinary-looking tooth and told them it belonged to a creature no one believed could even exist. Oh, and also, their maps were wrong.

Buckland dismissed it as the tooth of a large fish. Conybeare thought Mantell had analyzed the strata wrong (a common amateur mistake) and it was the tooth of a mammal.

Disheartened and rejected, Mantell took the tedious, tiring carriage ride back to his hometown. The next day, he woke up from his dreams and went back to his

ODE TO A PROFESSOR'S HAMMER

Poetry was a popular form of entertainment among nineteenth-century gentlemen, for better and for worse. William Conybeare wrote this little ditty for the Geological Society:

Ode to a Professor's Hammer

Hail to the hammer of science profound!
Beneath the storm of its thundering
  blows . . .
Mountains reluctant their story disclose . . .
The fossil dead that so long have slept,
And seen world after world into ruin swept,
Start at the sound
Of its fearful rebound.

real life as a simple country doctor.

No matter how hard he tried, he wrote, he could not overcome "the prejudice which the humble situation of my family naturally excites in the mind of the great."

THE TRAVELS OF THE TOOTH
PART 2: PARIS

Mantell was down, but not out. In 1823, he began to feel like perhaps things were turning around.

First came *The Gentleman's Magazine*. This was a popular magazine that heard about Mantell's homemade fossil museum and sent a reporter to write about it. Not only did this help boost the number of visitors to Mantell's house (much to his wife's dismay), but the article made particular mention of the massive fossils that Mantell believed belonged to a reptile. This was exactly the sort of legitimacy that Mantell was looking for.

The second lifeline came from Charles Lyell. After their initial meeting, Lyell was a firm believer in Mantell's ideas. He came to Mantell with an incredible proposal. He was traveling to France, and he had an invitation to see the great Cuvier. Would Mantell give him the tooth so he could show it to the Father of Paleontology?

The answer was obvious. In the world of paleontology, Cuvier could make or break a career, confirm or deny a discovery, conjure an extinct animal into existence with a single statement. The word of Cuvier was like the word of God. Mantell sent the tooth off with Lyell, but then all he could do was wait to hear the response.

Unfortunately for Mantell, this particular god enjoyed throwing the best parties in Paris. Cuvier was a celebrity. The French government had recognized his achievements by making him a baron. His parties were packed with politicians, intellectuals, and high-society women all mingling and basking in the glow of Cuvier's brilliance.

In hindsight, "late at night at a party" probably isn't the best time to get someone's scientific opinion on the existence on entirely new species. However, that was the only chance Lyell had, so he took it. In the middle of the party, Lyell unwrapped a handkerchief and showed the tooth to Cuvier.

The great man leaned forward to examine it . . .

His well-dressed admirers crowded around, waiting to be entertained by the great man's famously quick decisions. Mantell anxiously waited at his home, his entire career (and mental well-being) hanging on this moment.

. . . and then . . . Cuvier declared that it was a rhinoceros tooth and nothing more.

Then, he went back to the party and his guests.

It was crushing news, but that night Lyell dutifully mailed a letter to Mantell informing him of Cuvier's decision.

The next morning, however, Cuvier contacted Lyell and admitted that it had been rather late the night before, and his senses weren't at their sharpest. In fact, he told Lyell, he found the tooth *very* interesting.

For some unknown reason, though, Lyell never wrote a second letter. The only news that reached Mantell was Cuvier's rejection. Mantell had raised his hopes again only to have them crushed even lower. He'd sacrificed so much for his dream—the money, the countless hours. He'd become a stranger to his own family,

An older, plumper, more respected Georges Cuvier.

and it was all for nothing.

Mantell set his fossils aside. He put his pen away. His journal, normally bursting with his thoughts, fell silent. He couldn't bear to "record mementos of wretchedness."

That could easily have been how Mantell lived out the rest of his life—silent, wretched, anonymous. But then Mary Anning offered salvation.

STRANGER THINGS

If Gideon Mantell thought he was having a rough time, he had nothing on Mary Anning. Day after day, every day, she went to the cliffs—

Chip-chip-chip-

But she hadn't made any discoveries as big as her ichthyosaur in over a year. She and her family were on the brink of starvation. They began selling their furniture in order to survive.

They were only saved when one of their wealthy customers stepped in with an extraordinary act of charity. He sold his entire collection and gave them the profit. He wrote: "In truth [the Annings] found almost all [these] fine things. . . . I may never again possess what I am about to part with, yet in doing it I shall have the satisfaction of knowing that the money will be well applied."

The sale earned the Annings the equivalent of $39,000. Mary determined never to go hungry again, so she went back to the cliffs.

Chip-chip-chip-

When Cuvier first announced the existence of an ancient world, it was an empty place (except for a woolly mammoth or two), but as Mary burrowed into the cliffs of Lyme Regis, she began to fill its seas and sky. She unearthed hundreds, if not thousands, of smaller fossils.

She found the first pterosaur in England.

She found the first *Squaloraja* (a Jurassic-era cross between a shark and a ray, whose descendants—known as ghost sharks—are still alive today).

She found fossilized ink sacks in belemnites, linking them to modern cuttlefish and squid. Not only that, but she discovered that those ink sacks could be ground up and used to write. She wrote letters in 200-million-year-old fossil ink!

But she also knew that something more lay hidden in the cliffs. When Conybeare analyzed the original Anning ichthyosaur, he came across a handful of vertebrae that were different. He guessed that there must have been some "strange monster" that was trapped inside the cliffs along with *Ichthyosaurus*. It was simply waiting for a hammer and chisel to find it.

Chip-chip-chip-

And in 1823, that's exactly what Mary did.

Or rather, in 1823, she finished the job. The location was only accessible at low tide, so for a few hours every day, Mary stood with her feet and skirt in the freezing water as she worked to unearth the specimen. According to Buckland's diary, "It took Miss Anning ten years to extract the entire skeleton . . . from its watery grave."

It's hard to imagine the patience and self-control this required. At any point during this time, Mary could have carved out an individual bone and sold it for decent money. But despite poverty, hardship, and occasional brushes with actual hunger, she kept digging for the whole creature in the hope of finding something truly spectacular.

This wasn't just a skull or a few vertebrae. It was a 9-foot-long, fully intact "sea dragon," and its sheer weirdness made *Ichthyosaurus* pale in comparison. William Buckland described it as having a "head like a lizard, neck like a snake, body of a crocodile. . . ." Conybeare named it *Plesiosaurus* ("near lizard").

It was so bizarre that when Cuvier first saw Mary's illustration, he accused her of fakery. Other fossil hunters at the time were known to embellish their finds by gluing on extra bones to improve their value. Mary never did, even though her honesty cost her money.

Buckland and Conybeare made a special trip down to Lyme Regis to investigate the claim. When they wrote to Cuvier that it was genuine, a stunned Cuvier admitted (possibly for the first time in his life) that he was wrong.

The plesiosaur was given the royal treatment. Buckland and Conybeare wanted to present it as soon as possible to the Geological Society, so they arranged a special ship to transport the bones to London. Mary herself was left behind. She only left Lyme Regis once in her entire life.

However, the sale of the plesiosaur (for a little under $12,000 in today's

This fossil was a *Squaloraja* approx. 1.5 feet long. An actual *Squaloraja* is bigger, but Mary only found the tail later. Unfortunately, this illustration is all we have of Mary's discovery. The actual fossil was destroyed during Nazi bombing raids on London in World War II.

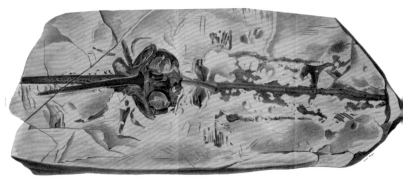

money) helped Mary slowly pull her way out of poverty. She even managed to buy a small shop, Anning's Fossil Depot.

To scientists, she was anonymous. But Mary knew that to science itself, she was a legend. Her neighbors had no idea the biggest names in science (like Cuvier) were visiting her shop. When the king of Saxony entered her store to make a purchase, Mary proudly declared, "I am well known throughout the whole of Europe."

But pride does not pay for food. Mary had a business to run. So every day she went back to the cliffs with her hammer and chisel and—

Chip-chip-chip-

—bit by bit, she worked to free the creatures that were trapped in the rocks, trapped in the times they lived in.

"THE GREAT LIZARD OF STONESFIELD"

The plesiosaur was such an exciting find that Conybeare arranged to present it to the Geological Society as soon as possible. The date was set for February 20, 1824.

Buckland also learned that at that same meeting he would be elected the new president of the Geological Society. With his typical showman's flair, he decided he should kick off his presidency by presenting something of his own.

After *six years* of waiting, William Buckland finally decided to present "the giant Lizard of Stonesfield." This would enter the existence of giant land reptiles into the official record of science.

When Mantell heard the news, all of his buried dreams came roaring back to life. This was a golden opportunity. No one had listened to his opinions about ancient reptiles, but they would have to listen to Buckland. And Mantell's collection of *Megalosaurus* teeth and bones would support Buckland's research. The Geological Society would *have* to pay attention to him now. Mantell packed his bags. He was heading back to London.

February 20 was going to be a momentous evening in the history of science, and Gideon Mantell wanted his piece of the glory.

Illustration of *Plesiosaurus* in letter from Mary Anning to Conybeare in 1823. She wrote: "I may venture to assure you it is the first and only one discovered in Europe." The letter demonstrates her business skills. She was negotiating the sale among three different clients and seeking a higher price.

PART 9

THE NIGHT OF TWO MONSTERS AND THE GREAT ÉCLAT

THE GEOLOGICAL SOCIETY MEETING
FEBRUARY 20, 1824

"With two monsters . . . and so crowded an audience, my first evening of taking the chair as President was one of great éclat." That is what William Buckland wrote about the evening he introduced *Megalosaurus* to the world.

The word "éclat" is a French term that means several things. It can mean "a moment of social success," but its literal meaning is "a flash of brilliant light."

In this particular case, both meanings are accurate. It was an evening of social success because Buckland was elected president of the Geological Society. As for the flash of brilliant light, that arrived at exactly 8:30 p.m.

That was the time that the lecture began. There were a little over 30 people crowded into the small room, but William Conybeare noted that the audience was "the largest I ever remember." This is a good indication of just how small the world of geology was at the time. In the entire country of England, only 30 or so people were aware of the incredible discoveries being made. Gideon Mantell was in attendance as well, having traveled all the way up from Sussex.

Conybeare began. He stood up and delivered his presentation on Anning's *Plesiosaurus*. While he spoke, William Buckland waited nervously in his chair. Despite his reputation as a gifted and charismatic speaker, William Buckland always had to work up the courage to speak. A friend noticed that "[William] feels very nervous in addressing large assemblies till he has once made them

laugh, and then he is entirely at ease."

However, this wasn't his classroom. He couldn't joke with his peers the same way he did with his students (charging at them with a hyena jaw and screaming at the top of his lungs). As the new president of the society, that simply wouldn't do.

The other reason for Buckland's nerves was that he still considered the fossil record of *Megalosaurus* incomplete. He would have preferred additional time to build a more complete skeleton, but the pressure had been slowly building on him to go public.

Ever since Cuvier had identified the Stonesfield bones as reptilian, in 1818, he'd written to Buckland several times asking Buckland to announce his findings. Cuvier wanted to include *Megalosaurus* in his next book, but the scientific societies honored a strict gentleman's code of ethics. Cuvier couldn't write about the creature until Buckland announced it first.

Despite Buckland's delay, the discovery was an open secret in the geological community. In 1822, Gideon Mantell's favorite author, James Parkinson, wrote a book about extinct animals in which he actually coined the name *Megalosaurus*, to describe the Stonesfield bones. But since he didn't have any more information to go on, he simply wrote, "It is hoped a description may shortly be given to the public."

The final push for Buckland might have been the article on Gideon Mantell in *The Gentleman's Magazine*. If Buckland waited any longer, he was at risk of someone else claiming the fame.

Buckland's instincts were spot-on. Presenting the two "monsters" together as a double feature made for a thrilling evening.

MONSTER #1

Conybeare regaled the members with the extraordinary details of the *Plesiosaurus*. It had "the teeth of the Crocodile . . . the ribs of a Chameleon, and the paddles of a Whale." It had 35 vertebrae in its neck!

For comparison, a giraffe and human both have 7. The extant animal (i.e., an animal that's still alive) with the most neck vertebrae on the planet are swans, which have up to 25. In other words, 35 was simply absurd.

Conybeare seemed genuinely concerned about its ability to defend itself. *Ichthyosaurus* was the only other

Clash of the Titans: ichthyosaur vs. plesiosaur.

sea creature they knew of, so he assumed the two were constantly locked in mortal combat. He spent a good amount of time comparing their fighting abilities.

Noting the plesiosaur's small head, Conybeare said, "[This] smallness of the head, and therefore of the teeth, must have rendered it a very unequal combatant against [*Ichthyosaurus*]. . . . It may perhaps have lurked in [shallow] water along the coast, concealed among the seaweed . . . a secure retreat from the assaults of dangerous enemies."

It was now time for the grand finale—the viewing. It was a suitably eerie event. The morning of the lecture, workers had struggled valiantly to carry the plesiosaur up the stairs into the lecture hall. But the framed specimen was so large (10 feet long and 6 feet wide) that it wouldn't fit up the stairs.

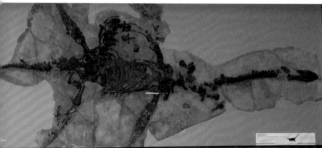

Mary Anning's *Plesiosaurus* at London's Natural History Museum, with grown human (author) and not-grown human (author's son) for scale.

They settled on storing it in a dark hallway on the first floor. The members of the society crowded together in the dark, using the lights of their flickering candles to get their first glimpse of the ancient beast.

As they filed back to the lecture hall, Conybeare was quite pleased with his performance. His speaking style was usually poor (he was "ungraceful" and "frightened the ladies"), but every geologist had learned a lesson from Buckland's presentation on the Kirkdale Cave. Geology was about making the past come alive, and Conybeare reckoned, "I made my beast roar as loud as Buckland's hyaenas."

MONSTER #2

Now, it was William Buckland's turn. He rose to give his lecture on what he called "the great fossil lizard of Stonesfield."

He started somewhat tentatively. "I am induced to lay before the Geological Society the . . . parts of the skeleton of an enormous fossil animal."

The word "induced" was perhaps Buckland's admission that he didn't think the skeleton was quite ready. In fact, he said, he was giving this talk "in the hope that" other people would come forward with "other parts of the same reptile."

This must have been music to Gideon Mantell's ears. In a bag at his feet were the massive thighbone and carnivorous tooth from his own collection. He must have spent the entire lecture silently urging Buckland to finish so he could have his turn at show-and-tell.

Buckland was a geologist, not an anatomist, and it showed in his analysis of the creature's body. For starters, "the Great Lizard" is not actually a lizard. All dinosaurs are, in fact, reptiles.

Some of the mistakes in his presentation were understandable. This was the first time anyone had tried to describe such a creature. Even Cuvier's contributions were wrong.

Buckland told the members that Cuvier used his famous "correlation of the parts" to estimate that the creature was 7 feet tall and 40 feet long. The prob-

lem was that Cuvier's theory didn't work with fossils this old. He compared fossil creatures to their modern cousins, but these creatures were so ancient that they had very little in common with the modern world. Scientists now estimate that *Megalosaurus* was approximately 20 feet long and weighed 2,000 pounds. These errors were only understood and corrected many years later.

For that evening, though, the overestimate of the size would have had a stunning effect on the audience. In nineteenth-century England, people were still entertained by the exotic sight of an elephant, so the idea of a carnivorous reptile twice that size was jaw dropping.

The "Great Lizard" was a truly unique creature for more than just its size. Its flesh-ripping 3.5-inch teeth were placed in the jaw like a reptile (with replacements lined up and ready to go), but its legs fit into its hips like a mammal. So instead of its legs splaying out to the side like a reptile, they descended straight down from its torso, like a bird or human.

MONSTER OF MERCY

Buckland, along with most geologists at the time, assumed that *Megalosaurus* lived at the same time as human beings and was wiped out by Noah's flood. Buckland was well aware that this created a few biblical problems.

If God was good, kind, and tried "to produce the greatest amount of enjoyment," why would He make a 40-foot-long, flesh-ripping terror-machine like *Megalosaurus*? Buckland was a devoutly religious man, so he wanted to find a way to make science and religion agree. Eventually, the ever-diplomatic Buckland came up with a creative solution. He said:

"It has pleased the Creator to give . . . to every creature upon the earth [an amount] of kindness to make the end of life to each individual as easy as possible. . . . By sudden destruction . . . the feeble and disabled are speedily relieved from suffering."

In other words, God showed His love by making *Megalosaurus* so ferocious that you wouldn't suffer if it ate you because it would kill you good and quick.

Mary Morland's illustration of the first *Megalosaurus* jawbone, published with Buckland's account of its discovery.

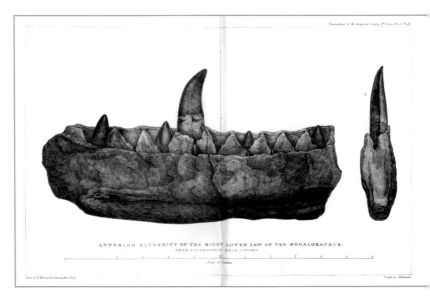

ANTERIOR EXTREMITY OF THE RIGHT LOWER JAW OF THE MEGALOSAURUS.

This creates the upright, bipedal (standing on two feet) stance that we associate with dinosaurs today.

Every ancient reptile discovered up until that point was an aquatic creature, so Buckland wasn't prepared to say that this was a fully land-based creature. He split the difference by declaring that it "was probably an amphibious animal."

Despite being labeled "amphibious," the fact that the creature obviously walked on land was incredible. Cuvier's pterodactyl flew in the sky. Anning's creatures swam in the seas. The more fossils scientists found, the more they realized that Cuvier's phrase, "an Age of Reptiles," was frighteningly accurate.

At a certain point in the past, giant reptiles existed in every ecosystem on Earth.

In one respect, Buckland wasn't as lucky as Conybeare. He didn't have a complete skeleton to help his audience visualize this spectacular creature. Instead, he passed around beautifully detailed illustrations that pleased him for a very different reason—they were drawn by an extraordinary young woman he had recently met.

Buckland had reached the ripe old age of 40 without marrying. He'd dedicated so much of his life to geology that no woman could compete for his attention. At least, not until two years earlier when he found himself sitting in a carriage across from a young woman . . . who was reading the latest book by Georges Cuvier.

After a brief conversation, Buckland had learned that her name was Mary Morland. She was the adopted daughter of Sir Christopher Pegge, his old anatomy professor at Oxford and the man

❧ LOVE ROCKS ❧

For a geologist, asking someone to sketch your fossils is clearly the most romantic gesture it's possible to make. Miraculously, Mary was as much of a fossil buff as Buckland and she gladly accepted the job. She became his lifelong illustrator and research assistant.

One year later, she accepted his hand in marriage as well, and they eventually had nine children together.

who bought the *Megalosaurus* jawbone in the first place!

Once Buckland learned that Mary was a trained anatomical artist, he asked if she would illustrate his entire *Megalosaurus* fossil collection. She agreed and created one of the most well-known fossil drawings in science.

Buckland wrapped up his lecture with one final piece of business. He had to enter the scientific name of the "Great Lizard" into the official record. In his typically generous style, he made sure to pay tribute to those who helped him:

"I have ventured, in concurrence with my friend and fellow-labourer, the Rev. W. Conybeare, to assign to it the name Megalosaurus."

When a lecture at the society was finished, it was a common practice for other members to offer comments. Gideon Mantell did more than that. He stood and told the members that he could support Buckland's claims. He then produced a femur that was twice the size of Buckland's Stonesfield bones.

If any member of the Geological Society ever gasped in shock, this would have been the time for it. Using Cuvier's (again, incorrect) calculations, they estimated the creature would have been 60 to 70 feet long—a carnivore that was "little short of the largest whales[!]"

The evening was a smashing success. Conybeare wrote that "it was one of the pleasantest public meetings I have ever attended."

It is not hard to see why. Every person in the room that night surely felt that they had reached a tipping point in their field of science. The past was beginning to open and spill out its secrets, and the truth was more awe inspiring than anything they could have imagined.

Now that the evidence was laid out, understanding the past no longer required someone to be a visionary, like Cuvier or Mantell. Every scientist around the world held the key to unlocking the existence of other dinosaurs.

THE SIX BLIND MEN AND THE ELEPHANT
PART 3

In the story of the six blind men, they examine an elephant to understand it better.

The story in this book is slightly different because no one went looking for dinosaurs. You can't search for something if you don't even know it exists. But for thousands of years, humans groped blindly in the dark, trying to understand what the bones underground could possibly mean. They guessed, and got things wrong and got things right, and bit by bit, they put their ideas together, and on February 20, 1824, in a flash of brilliant light, the existence of a dinosaur was revealed.

It was an evening of great éclat.

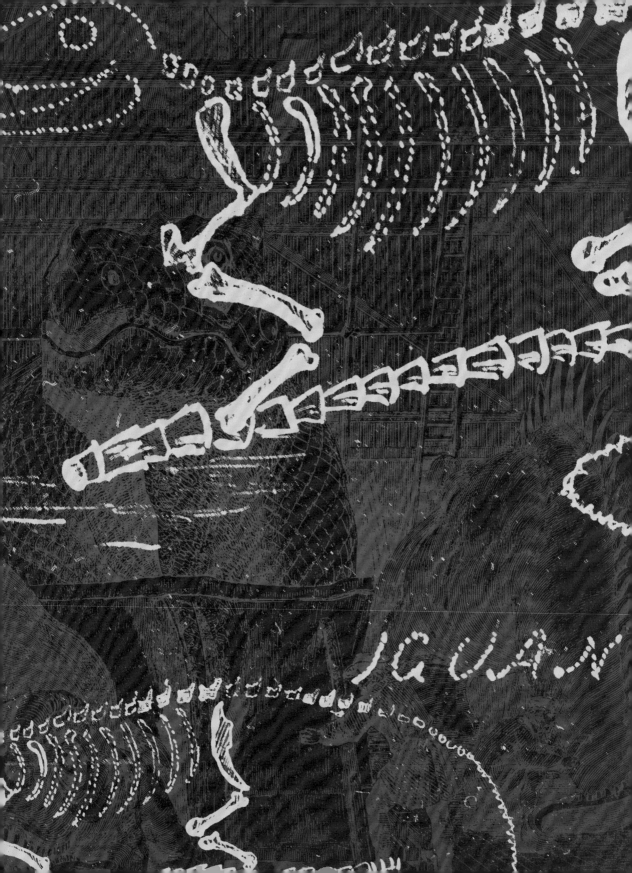

THE FIRST DINOSAUR

"A NEW ANIMAL"

Megalosaurus may have been the first dinosaur discovered, but no one knew it yet because it was the only one discovered. Dinosaurs are an entire class of animal, which now contains approximately 800 species (with more being found every year). But since *Megalosaurus* was the first of its kind, Buckland, Mantell, and others had no other species to compare it to. In fact, after the announcement of the existence of *Megalosaurus* it would take another 18 years before the creation of the word "dinosaur."

That process was set in motion that very same evening that Buckland introduced *Megalosaurus* to the Geological Society, and it began with Gideon Mantell.

By supporting Buckland with fossils from his own collection, Mantell raised his reputation. For years, he'd hoped to have Buckland view his fossil collection. He finally got his wish. Buckland and Conybeare both traveled to his house and reassessed the tooth that Mantell had showed them a year earlier. They agreed with his theory, but there was only one person whose opinion truly mattered— Georges Cuvier. He was the ultimate authority.

Buckland and Conybeare encouraged Mantell to write another letter to Cuvier, with their backing. This time, Mantell got a very different reply.

The Frenchman wrote back, "Might we not have here a new animal, an herbivorous reptile?"

Mantell rejoiced. That one sentence from Cuvier was enough to open every door that had been previously closed to

Mantell. But before he could announce his discovery at one of the scientific societies, he had to identify what type of animal it might be. To do this, he traveled to the Royal College of Surgeons.

The college's Hunterian Museum had over 20,000 animal specimens. Mantell spent hours trying in vain to find a tooth that even vaguely resembled his fossil.

His search soon attracted the attention of a young assistant in the museum who had just finished preserving some samples brought back from Barbados. The animals of the West Indies are completely different from those in Europe, and among those samples was something that no one in

Modern iguana. Now imagine this nine feet tall.

The massive collection of curiosities at the Hunterian Museum, Royal College of Surgeons.

England had ever seen before—an iguana, an herbivorous reptile.

The teeth matched almost exactly (besides the fact that Mantell's tooth was 10 times larger!). Mantell had found what he was looking for. A modern creature that proved his imagined creature was possible.

Now he had to name it. Mantell took his cue from Cuvier's mastodon research and called his creature *Iguanodon* ("iguana tooth").

Mantell was confident that his moment had arrived. He wrote, "I shall ride on the back of my *Iguanodon* into the temple of immortality!"

In a small gesture of defiance to the Geological Society that had ignored him for so long, Mantell introduced *Iguanodon* at the more prestigious Royal Society. In recognition of his work, the Royal Society accepted Mantell as their newest member. In 1825, Mantell traveled to the Royal Society's home in London and there, "with no small degree of pleasure . . . I placed my name in the Charter Book which contained that of Sir Isaac Newton. . . ."

Mantell had achieved his lifelong dream, but it had come at a cost.

T.H. Shephard.

E. Radclyffe.

Hunterian Museum.

Royal College of Surgeons.

THE PRICE OF GLORY

Mantell's obsession with fossils had nearly bankrupted him. He had ignored his family and pushed his body to its limits. He knew this and accepted it as part of the cost of his success. What he didn't know was that his success would cost him even more.

He had always hoped to attract visitors to the collection in his home. After his discovery of *Iguanodon*, that wish came true. As many as 100 to 200 visitors a day came to his house—some of whom were so enthusiastic about Mantell's collection that they stayed until two o'clock in the morning. Unfortunately, the crowds drove his patients away from his practice, and he considered it ungentlemanly to charge his visitors a fee.

The family was soon flat broke.

Somewhat understandably, Mantell's wife, Mary, decided she'd had enough. She ended their marriage. By 1829, Mantell confessed that he was "worried to death with visitors . . . this notoriety is a curse."

That wasn't Mantell's only problem. Inspired by his success, wealthy amateur collectors began visiting Mantell's regular quarries and paid the quarrymen far greater sums than he could afford. Mantell was cut off from his fossil supply. He was forced to work with scraps. Literally.

In 1832, workers in one of his regular quarries, Tilgate Forest, were blasting rock when they noticed some fossils inside the rubble. Whatever the specimen had been, it was now shattered into over 50 pieces. No wealthy collector would pay for a pile of shattered rocks, so the workers offered it to Mantell at a discount price.

He accepted the challenge. Over the next few weeks, he pieced together the jigsaw puzzle to form a 4½-foot block of stone. Then, he began to chisel away.

It was an especially difficult specimen to work on because strange spikes kept appearing at unexpected angles. But

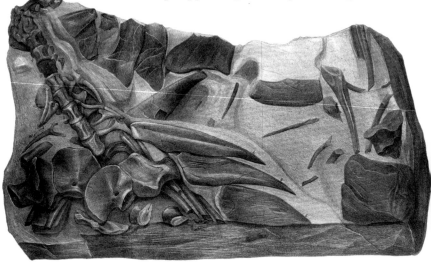

The jumble of fossils that is *Hylaeosaurus*.

slowly, carefully, he managed to reveal something completely new.

It required another incredible leap of imagination by Mantell to understand the purpose of those spikes. They were a form of defensive protection that ran along the body of the creature. Mantell had discovered the first armored dinosaur.

At another meeting of the Geological Society, he named it for the quarry where it was found, *Hylaeosaurus* ("forest lizard"). *Hylaeosaurus* never reached the level of fame of some of the other early discoveries, but most people recognize its cousin, *Ankylosaurus*. When Mantell finished his presentation, the members gave him a warm round of applause.

Science now recognized three giant, prehistoric land reptiles—*Megalosaurus, Iguanodon,* and *Hylaeosaurus*—and Gideon Mantell had discovered two of them. This is often considered the "golden age of geology." Discoveries of dramatic new creatures were coming fast. The news began to spread, exciting members of the public to take weekend jaunts into the countryside with hammers and chisels.

Geology was the most exciting science of the time and everyone, it seemed, wanted to find the next creature.

But no one—absolutely *no* one—burned with more ambition than a young anatomy student who was sitting in the audience that evening, watching as Mantell soaked in the applause.

That young man's name was Richard Owen. He would make the final step required in the discovery of dinosaurs, and he wouldn't let anyone stop him.

RICHARD OWEN
[THE SCIENTIST]

Richard Owen was born in the town of Lancaster, in the north of England. Although his family wasn't wealthy, they had enough money to send him to a good school. It didn't do Owen much good. He had a terrible temper and he got into frequent fights in school. His disciplinary problems prevented him from attending university, so his father had the same idea as Gideon Mantell's father. He apprenticed his son to a local doctor.

Richard Owen trying to look cool, but ending up sort of creepy.

Mantell's education as a country doctor began with home births and aching teeth, but Owen's education had a much darker quality. Lancaster was home to a stone dungeon of a jail, and Owen's new boss performed the autopsy on any prisoner who died inside its walls.

At first, Owen was terrified by these dissections. But as he got used to it, he became fascinated with anatomy. He excelled so fast in his studies and abilities with a knife that he was accepted at a number of medical schools. He eventually moved to London to train to become a naval surgeon, but his interest in research sidetracked those plans.

He took a job working at the Royal College of Surgeons' Hunterian Museum (the same place where Gideon Mantell found his iguana). Their specimen collection was one of the largest in the world, but when Owen arrived to start work, it was in chaos.

Every museum needs its collection analyzed, noted, and catalogued. Otherwise, it's just a pile of random bones. Most of the specimens *did* originally have notes made by the original collector, a famous surgeon named John Hunter. However, Hunter died suddenly, and those notes disappeared. They were taken by his brother-in-law, a dull-witted aristocrat-turned-hobby-scientist named Sir Everard Home.

To advance his own career, Home published the important parts of his dead brother-in-law's papers under his own name. As for the unimportant papers (the catalogue of the Hunterian Museum, for example), he covered his tracks by burning some . . . and using the rest as toilet paper!

So by sheer chance, Owen received an education very similar to George Cuvier's. They both apprenticed at famous museums with vast collections that needed someone who was young, talented, and energetic enough to put it in order.

Owen often became so immersed in his research that he brought his work home with him, unaware of how it looked to the outside world. One evening, he walked home with one of his specimens in a brown paper bag. It was the severed head of a sailor.

Unfortunately, the bag slipped out of his hand and the head rolled downhill and through the front

door of someone's home. Owen ran in, scooped up the head, and ran off without saying a word before the family inside the house could react. For weeks after that, rumors of ghost sailors and the devil floated around town.

Perhaps to avoid such problems again, Owen had specimens delivered straight to his home. His wife (clearly a woman of great patience) often came home and found dead animals in her front hallway. One time, it was an entire rhinoceros; another time it was the brains of an elephant. Apparently, that last one was too much even for her. She had to open every window in the house to clear away the smell of rotting brains.

Owen's similarities to Cuvier didn't stop there. He was soon able to identify an animal from a single bone. Within the first two years of working at the museum, he published 28 papers detailing new discoveries in anatomy. His intellectual abilities were so similar to Cuvier's that when Cuvier himself came to visit the Hunterian Museum, Owen was given the responsibility of showing the great man around. Cuvier was so impressed that he invited Owen to come work as his assistant at the National Museum of Natural History in Paris.

A CUVIER FOR THE UK

This was an interesting time in the science of geology. It was beginning to split into two. Originally, geology was the study of everything related to Earth's past—rocks, gems, fossils, whatever was found underground. But once geologists figured out that these fossils came from ancient creatures, they were out of their depth.

Geologists understood rocks, not biology (this was obvious from the mistakes Buckland made in his paper on *Megalosaurus*). To understand how to take a few bones and translate them into an entire creature required a knowledge of anatomy. Cuvier is the Father of Paleontology because he had these skills, but he lived in France.

Meanwhile, England was resource-rich, but knowledge-poor. Because of England's unique geology and the global reach of its empire, English scientists had access to an incredible number of fossils. Unidentified bones were coming out of the ground and arriving on ships from around the world every month. But England had no one with the skills of Cuvier.

Before phones or the Internet, if English geologists like Buckland and Conybeare wanted a fossil identified, they had to mail illustrations to Cuvier (if there wasn't a war raging) or wait for his occasional visits to England. This was part of the reason that the identification of the *Megalosaurus* bones took so long.

When Owen returned from his apprenticeship in anatomy in Paris, he had exactly the skill set that England needed.

Waiting for him was an enormous amount of unexamined specimens, ready to be discovered.

Over the course of his career, Owen wrote over 600 papers detailing new discoveries in biology and anatomy. He became one of the most decorated English scientists in history. He received France's highest scientific award. Queen Victoria gifted him a large house in London.

He was placed in charge of the Hunterian Museum and the British Museum. He was even knighted—Sir Richard Owen.

By the 1840s, most of the original generation of geologists were fading. Cuvier had died in 1832. Buckland left Oxford in 1845 to become dean of Westminster Abbey (England's most important

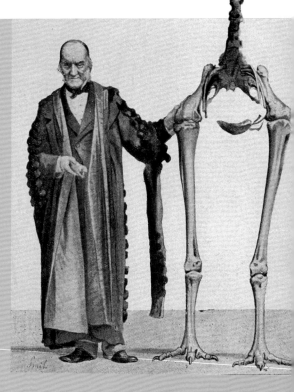

THE ENGLISH CUVIER

In 1839, Richard Owen would have made Cuvier proud. He received a 15-centimeter fragment of a femur from New Zealand (in his hand in the picture on the right). From that single bone he guessed that at some point in the past, New Zealand was home to a flightless bird the size of a giant ostrich (known as a moa).

This was such a preposterous idea that he was widely ridiculed, until three years later when a complete set of moa bones was found in New Zealand . . . *by Gideon Mantell's oldest son!*

This feat was reported widely in the press. Not only did it elevate Owen's status, but it raised the profile of paleontology in the public eye. Astronomy had the ability to predict the future with the arrival of eclipses and comets. Now the new science of paleontology seemed as if it could conjure up the past.

church), and Conybeare remained a country minister. The only person who was still active and whose achievements rivaled those of Owen was Gideon Mantell.

This was a problem for Gideon Mantell.

Over the course of Owen's career, he had developed a nasty habit of destroying anyone who got in his way. Gideon Mantell didn't know it yet, but he was in Owen's way.

RICHARD OWEN
THE FIEND

Every biography written about Richard Owen has to deal with two separate ideas:

1) Richard Owen was, without a doubt, an incredibly talented scientist.

2) Richard Owen was, without a doubt, a horrible human being.

Owen's talent for science was only matched by his ability to play politics. At every turn in his career he schmoozed the right people to put him in a position of power. Besides managing several museums, he was on the advisory board for the Geological Society and the Royal Society. In each case, he used his power to destroy his rivals.

A biologist at the Hunterian challenged some of Owen's ideas . . . so

Owen barred the man from the museum. Without access to his specimens and research, the man's career was finished. He lost his students and slid into poverty and anonymity, exactly where Owen wanted him.

> ## "It's a pity a man so talented should be so dastardly and envious."
> —GIDEON MANTELL

In 1845, an amateur biologist discovered a new form of belemnite (a fossil shell). Owen stole his discovery and claimed it for himself. This "discovery" earned Owen the Royal Medal, one of the Royal Society's highest honors. This would have been the high point of any scientist's career, but Owen always wanted more praise, more awards, more fame.

It's no wonder that he turned his attention to *Megalosaurus* and *Iguanodon*. These massive reptiles were the most exciting discoveries of the early nineteenth century. The problem for Owen was that Gideon Mantell was rightly acknowledged as the foremost expert on the subject. So Owen began a very steady, very deliberate campaign to destroy the career that Mantell had worked so hard to build.

At first, Mantell had no idea that

anything was afoot. He was busy with his own share of troubles. To capitalize on his newfound fame, he'd moved to London, but it only made things worse. His medical practice struggled, his wife did not return, his older children moved away, and tragically, his youngest daughter died in his arms from tuberculosis. Amid all this turmoil, he was still trying to work on his own research.

But he suddenly found that his papers were getting rejected by the Royal Society. Without any of his new studies being published in the science journals, it appeared as if his ideas had run out. Anonymous newspaper and magazine articles began criticizing his previous work. Mantell was baffled by the bad luck that seemed to plague him, but the source of the trouble soon became clear.

Richard Owen began publishing articles that plagiarized Mantell's research. He even tried to take credit for a creature that Mantell discovered. This last act was so blatant that the society took the rare step of warning Owen about his behavior. For his part, Mantell found himself baffled by Owen's need to rob glory from "anyone [who] put a foot upon the lowest step of his throne."

The final straw came when the Royal Society proposed giving Mantell the Royal Medal to honor his lifetime of work. Owen, for no reason except spite, argued vehemently against it.

"All Mantell has done," Owen told the award committee, "was collect the fossils and let others work them out!"

Fortunately, both William Buckland and Charles Lyell wrote letters of support for Mantell, and the society voted in favor. At the award ceremony, Owen offered Mantell a token handshake but Mantell stiffly refused and turned away.

Owen attacked Mantell's ideas because that was the one area in which he could compete. Owen didn't come from the original generation of geologists like Buckland, Conybeare, and Mantell, who spent every free moment in a quarry. Owen spent his life as an academic working indoors. He would never discover new fossils out in the field, so he had to rely on his analytical powers.

Owen clearly felt that any new ideas that contradicted Mantell's research on *Iguanodon* (Mantell's greatest discovery) were a point in his favor. This is the great difficulty in writing about Richard Owen. He was clearly trying to tear Mantell down and take credit for himself. But on the other hand, his research actually paid off. Owen found something remarkable.

"I WOULD PROPOSE THE NAME OF DINOSAURIA"

Cuvier re-created the mastodon by looking at similarities and differences in elephants' teeth. Owen re-created dinosaurs

JOINED AT THE HIP

Since the first dinosaur hunters were working with such a small fossil record, many of their ideas are now outdated. However, the importance of dinosaurs' hips has remained. Modern paleontologists classify dinosaurs into two groups: "bird-hipped" (ornithischians) and "lizard-hipped" (saurischians).

The main difference is the angle at which their legs join their hips. Bird-hipped dinosaurs (like *Iguanodon, Hylaeosaurus,* and *Triceratops*) have their legs set at a backward angle. That provides more room for the abdomen and intestines, which are needed to digest plant material. That is why ornithischians tend to be herbivores.

Lizard-hipped dinosaurs (like *Megalosaurus, Tyrannosaurus rex,* and *Velociraptor*) have their legs pointed forward from the hip. That creates stronger legs and faster running, which increases their ability to catch prey. That is why saurischians tend to be carnivores.

It's important to note, however, that there are many, many exceptions to these rules. For instance, some saurischians are herbivores. In fact, evolution has created so many variations of dinosaur that some paleontologists are now suggesting entirely new ways to classify them. Who knows—current paleontologists may one day be as outdated as the original dinosaur hunters.

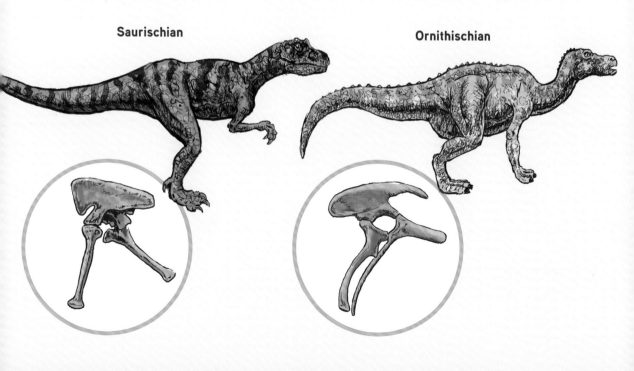

Saurischian

Ornithischian

by looking at their hips.

Owen observed that *Megalosaurus*, *Iguanodon*, and *Hylaeosaurus* all share a similar body structure. The first five vertebrae of their lower spine are fused together where they attach to the hips. These fused vertebrae strengthen the spine and helped them support their massive weight.

Nowadays, scientists know that there are two different hip structures to dinosaurs (usually referred to as "bird hips" and "lizard hips"). Not all dinosaurs have the five fused vertebrae, but by pure luck, the only three ancient reptiles known at that point shared that feature.

On August 2, 1841, Owen gave a lecture to a roomful of scientific luminaries. William Buckland himself attended to hear what England's number-one anatomist had to say about his *Megalosaurus*. Owen explained his findings, but it took him a full year of additional thinking before he published his thoughts. So it was in 1842 that he introduced the word "dinosaur" to the world.

"Dinosaur"—the name is famous, but it's actually a rather odd quirk of history. It means "terrible lizard," but Owen knew very well that dinosaurs are not lizards at all. They are reptiles. Perhaps he did this to keep the concept simple, since names like *Mosasaurus*, *Plesiosaurus*, and *Megalosaurus* were already well known.

> "[There is] sufficient ground for establishing a distinct tribe or suborder of Saurian Reptiles, for which I would propose the name of Dinosauria."
>
> —RICHARD OWEN

We also know that many dinosaurs weren't in the least bit terrifying. Some of them were only one foot high, a few pounds, covered with feathers, and feasted on nothing more gruesome than bugs. It just so happened that the only three dinosaurs that had been discovered back

Titanosaur and Hummingbird-osaur

of the carnivorous *Megalosaurus*, genuinely terrifying).

The idea of dinosaurs was a breakthrough similar to the Kirkdale Cave. Since *Megalosaurus*, *Iguanodon*, and *Hylaeosaurus* were all connected, this demonstrated that they were part of a much larger ecosystem. It promised that more dinosaurs were out there in the world just waiting to be discovered.

Considering the vast differences in the first three—a carnivore, an herbivore, and one covered in armor—people could only imagine what other strange creatures they might find. (Could they have imagined that the largest dinosaurs we now know

of are the titanosaurs, which reached 120 feet long and weigh 70 tons? Or that hummingbirds are considered a form of dinosaur as well?)

Despite this, dinosaurs didn't immediately leap from the halls of science into popular culture.

At that point, the concept of a "dinosaur" was nothing more than a few bones, a scientific paper on vertebrae, and an idea. It was such a radical and dramatic concept that for the idea to take root in the general public, people needed to be able to *see* what scientists were imagining.

They got that chance a decade later on the largest stage in England.

THE CRYSTAL PALACE

Half a *million* people gathered in London's Hyde Park on May 1, 1851. They were there to see Queen Victoria unveil the Crystal Palace.

It was an architectural wonder, a 20-acre building entirely covered in glass . . . 300,000 panels of glass, to be exact. The crowd's sense of awe must have mixed with a little unease. One newspaper worried that if the glass broke, "thousands of ladies will be cut into mincemeat."

The purpose of the exhibition was to show off the "very best that human ingenuity and cultivated art and science could inspire." It was the first World's Fair but, in truth, it was a celebration of Victorian England and the global might of the British Empire.

There were over 100,000 exhibits spread across 11 miles of stands. There was the world's largest diamond, the world's largest telescope, a knife with 1,851 blades, a weaving machine controlled by the earliest form of computer, a barometer made of leeches(!), and perhaps most importantly for modern readers, the world's first flushing toilet.

Despite the massive effort that went into building all of this, the exhibition was only scheduled to last for six months before it was torn down. But in that time, 6 million people (one-third of Britain's entire population) visited the exhibit. It

was so stunningly popular that the organizers decided to build a permanent copy of the Crystal Palace in an undeveloped area in the south of London.

The new location offered the designers far more room to work with, over 200 acres. They decided to dedicate a section

The Great Exhibition at the Crystal Palace, 1851.

of the park to the achievements of English geology. And what could be more visually spectacular than geology's most recent discovery?

They called it the Dinosaur Court, and it became the world's very first theme park. It would feature 33 life-size models of the various ancient creatures known at the time—*Megalosaurus*, *Megatherium*, *Mosasaurus* . . . most of the creatures featured in this book. There would be a tidal pond with machines raising and lowering the water level so the aquatic creatures

Interior of the Crystal Palace. Incredibly, this was just one small portion of the building.

like *Ichthyosaurus* and *Plesiosaurus* could mysteriously appear and disappear from view. They even included an exhibit of strata to show exactly where each animal had come from in Earth's past.

To build the models, they hired Benjamin Waterhouse Hawkins, a talented zoological artist who had worked closely with Charles Darwin. But the real challenge came with visualizing the creatures.

How do you imagine a complete dinosaur based only on a handful of bones?

Mary Anning uncovered complete skeletons of *Plesiosaurus* and *Ichthyosaurus*, but the fossil record for dinosaurs was woefully incomplete. It was a challenge that required someone with detailed expertise in dinosaur anatomy. The committee offered the job to Gideon Mantell.

By that time, Mantell was the leading dinosaur expert in the world. Since his discovery of *Hylaeosaurus*, he had found two more dinosaurs, meaning he had discovered four of the five dinosaurs known to science! Mantell even uncovered the first sauropod (the largest dinosaurs on Earth). He had written 67 books and 48 scientific papers for the Royal Society. More importantly, sometime around 1834, Mantell drew a rough sketch of what he thought his *Iguanodon* might look like.

The sketch (below) is a milestone in the history of art and science that is not well enough known or celebrated. It's the very first time that a human visualized what a dinosaur might look like.

Mantell was perfect for the Crystal Palace job. Unfortunately, his personal life had taken a turn for the worse. His obsessive pursuit of dinosaurs had hurt his medical practice. Few patients wanted to see a doctor who was more famous for his work on dead animals than living humans. He earned some money by giving public lectures on the *Iguanodon*, but not enough.

On top of that, Mantell was in nearly constant pain. He had struggled his whole life with a curvature of the spine, but that condition was made dramatically worse in October of 1841.

While traveling to see a patient, he fell off his carriage and got tangled in the horses' reins. The horses panicked and dragged him down the cobblestone street for hundreds of yards. From that moment on, he experienced spasms of pain throughout his body every single day. Simply moving around his house was excruciating.

It's hard to imagine how Mantell felt the day he was offered the job at Crystal Palace. They wanted him to create massive life-size models of his greatest discoveries and place them on the grandest stage in London. They wanted him to introduce dinosaurs to the world.

This was Mantell's dream come true.

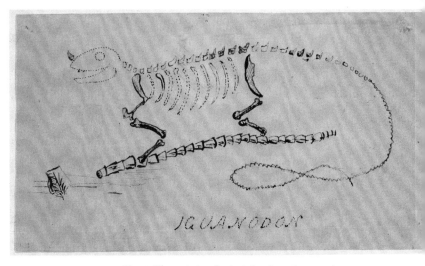

Mantell's notebook sketch of an *Iguanodon*. Historians argue about what Mantell was trying to do with its feet, which seem to blend in to the branch. But it's possible that feet are just really hard to draw and Mantell gave up.

He had sacrificed his entire life to achieve a moment like this . . . but the pain in his body was so intense that he had to turn the job down.

"In truth," he wrote, "I am used up."

So the committee offered the job to the next best qualified candidate, Mantell's archenemy, Richard Owen.

Older Mantell. Though he is smiling, his gaunt cheeks show that his personal troubles have begun to take a toll.

"MR. WATERHOUSE HAWKINS REQUESTS THE HONOR . . ."

Of the millions of dinosaurs that lived in the past, only a small fraction were preserved as fossils. Of those fossils, only a small fraction have been discovered. The job of Benjamin Waterhouse Hawkins, the artist and sculptor hired to create the theme park, was to fill in the gaps in the fossil record.

To do that, he first made sure to obtain precise information about the fossils that *were* known. He sent letters to Buckland, Conybeare, and others requesting absolutely precise measurements of their fossils. He traveled to the Ashmolean, the Geological Society, and the Hunterian Museum to examine them up close. Then, with Owen's help, Cuvier's laws of anatomy, and many hours working with clay models, Hawkins began to fill in the unknown. He became the first person to build a dinosaur.

In his workshop, he began to build fragments of bone into fully fleshed-out creatures.

Despite Hawkins's obsessive attention to measurements, he wasn't building science models. His job was to entertain, to draw the public into a prehistoric world

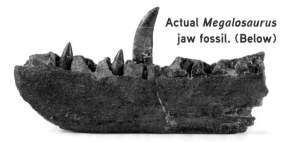

Actual *Megalosaurus* jaw fossil. (Below)

Hawkins's finished model of the *Megalosaurus* head. (Right)

The workshop of Benjamin Waterhouse Hawkins, 1853. (Opposite)

Two *Iguanodons* on Dinosaur Island, Crystal Palace. Each is over 10 feet tall.

and show dinosaurs as living creatures. So he set them in active poses, rearing their heads out of the water, climbing up a tree, or resting a claw lazily on a branch.

Because these were the very first representations of dinosaurs, there were bound to be some mistakes. He was using a fossil record that was far less complete than what we have today. This is a theme that runs through the history of paleontology. Modern paleontologists constantly revise their ideas about dinosaurs whenever they find new evidence.

Some of these mistakes were unavoidable. For instance, Gideon Mantell found a spike that he knew belonged to *Iguanodon*, but since it wasn't connected to the rest of the skeleton, he had no clue what sort of body part it could be. Both Mantell and Owen guessed that it went on the nose like a rhinoceros horn, so that's where Hawkins put it on the Crystal Palace *Iguanodon* (pictured above). It was only in 1878, when a complete *Iguanodon* skeleton was found in Belgium, that paleontologists discovered where the spike truly belonged—on the claw, like a thumb.

There was another mistake, however, that could have been avoided. After decades of thinking about *Iguanodon*, Mantell (correctly) guessed that its front limbs were smaller, and thus used for grasping. This meant that *Iguanodon* could stand on its hind legs—the posture that is familiar to modern dinosaur fans.

Richard Owen refused to accept any idea that came from Mantell, so the Crystal Palace Dinosaurs are famously posed like mammals, standing on all four legs.

This proved to be a huge challenge for Hawkins. He wrote in his notebook that making something that heavy stand on four legs was like "building a house upon four columns."

Hawkins had to be an engineer as much as an artist. He worked with 30 *tons* of clay, 600 bricks, 900 tiles, 38 casks of cement, 90 casks of stone, and 100 feet of iron. And that was just for the *Iguanodon*.

Hawkins prepped models in his workshop for an entire year before he began construction in the park. His project was so eagerly anticipated that Queen Victoria herself made a sneak visit to get the first glimpse at the beasts. Much to Hawkins's relief, she approved wholeheartedly. Despite the anatomical mistakes, Hawkins's artistry shined through—from the massive musculature of the large animals to the graceful curves of the aquatic creatures' necks to the finely detailed scales that cover each body. Hawkins made them come alive.

Six months before the official unveiling, he decided to show off his work by throwing a New Year's Eve party and inviting "the leading scientific men of the country."

For invitations, he drew an image of

The plesiosaur, mosasaur, and ichthyosaur on Dinosaur Island.

a pterodactyl, and on its wings, he wrote, "Mr. Waterhouse Hawkins requests the honor of [your] company in the mould of the *Iguanodon* at the Crystal Palace on the evening of December the 31st at five o'clock."

The 21 gentlemen who received the invitation must have been a bit curious about what it meant to attend a party "in the mould of the *Iguanodon*," but at 5:00 p.m. on December 31, 1853, they all arrived at what was now known as Crystal Palace Park. Dressed in their finest dinner attire, they strolled through the park to a tent that had been specially set up for the occasion. When they entered, they saw that the invitation was not exaggerating. There was a grand table set for a gourmet meal *inside* the hollow body of the *Iguanodon*.

THE JOLLY OLD BEAST

Food and wine and congratulations flowed that evening.

The gentlemen at the gathering actually had no idea how successful the exhibit would prove to be. On its first day it received 40,000 visitors. Over the next decade, the Crystal Palace Dinosaurs would become one of the most popular tourist sites in the world, averaging 2 million visitors a year.

The first dinosaur came from the Stonesfield quarries, but Crystal Palace Park was the place where the idea and images of dinosaurs began to enter popular culture.

The Dinosaur Court was such a hit that Hawkins built miniature models of the dinosaurs to sell as souvenirs. Mini dinosaur models made their way onto children's windowsills and shelves all over England. The dinosaurs were so visually exciting that they became popular with cartoonists and artists, who spread their images in newspapers and magazines. Dinosaurs soon began to appear in popular fiction.

But the partygoers weren't thinking that far into the future. That night, inside the *Iguanodon*, they were

The invitation created by Hawkins for his *Iguanodon* New Year's party, 1853.

Sketch of the New Year's party made that evening by a newspaper artist.

celebrating one of the greatest triumphs in the history of science—the discovery of the dinosaur.

These creatures had vanished 65 million years ago and now . . . these gentlemen were eating an eight-course meal inside of one!

The dinner guests raised a toast to Richard Owen, who was seated at the head of the table (quite literally) in the *Iguanodon*'s head. But hanging on signs over the table were the names of the other people responsible for solving the mystery of the dinosaur.

There was Cuvier, who proved that extinct animals existed. Buckland, who presented the idea to the world. Mantell, who imagined how fantastically weird they could be. And Owen, who found the thread that linked them all together.

But there was no mention of Dr. Parkinson, who first named *Megalosaurus*. Or Conybeare, who helped Buckland analyze the bones. And of course, Mary Anning's name was nowhere to be seen (even though she'd discovered three of the beasts in the park's display). Then again, the discovery of dinosaurs was such a monumental achievement that there wasn't enough room in the entire tent to display the names of all the people who contributed to the effort.

Dinosaur Island, Crystal Palace

People like William Smith, James Hutton, Dr. Plot, Nicolaus Steno, the Tradescants, the thousands of curiosity collectors who gathered the fossils together, and the countless anonymous miners and quarrymen who dug in the ground to earn a day's pay but uncovered scenes from Earth's deep time.

The idea was too big, too incredible, for any one person to solve. It took hundreds of years and thousands of people to build the dinosaurs of Crystal Palace, and for the Lost World to be reborn.

There is no precise record of what was said that evening. Perhaps the partygoers raised a toast to every one of those fine people. It was a New Year's Eve party, after all. We do know that when the food and drinks finally ran out, the guests merrily stumbled out into the cool night air and made their way to their waiting carriages.

As they walked together through the park, they burst out in a song they had written just for the occasion. Hawkins reported, "[Their] chorus was so loud and enthusiastic that you could almost believe there roared a herd of Iguanodons."

They sang:

"The jolly old beast is not deceased
There's life in him again!
ROOAARR!"

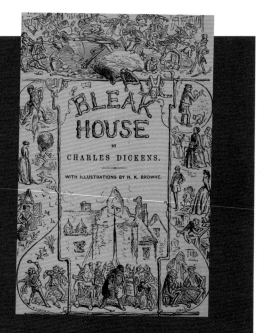

FIRST DINOSAUR IN FICTION

Megalosaurus wasn't just the first dinosaur to be named and described by science. It was also the first dinosaur to appear in fiction. It made its entrance on the very first page of Charles Dickens's 1853 novel, *Bleak House*: "... it would not be wonderful to meet a Megalosaurus, forty feet long or so, waddling like an elephantine lizard up Holborn Hill."

EPILOGUE

NICOLAUS STENO
1638-1686

By the time Nicolaus Steno made pioneering advances in anatomy, geology, and paleontology, he was only 31 years old. One of the great "What ifs?" in science is to ponder what other discoveries Steno could have made in his life, but we will never know.

In 1675, he left the natural sciences to become a Catholic priest. The church sent him to northern Germany, far from the Italian coast where he had made so many of his breakthroughs. Steno took a vow of poverty. He wore clothes that were too thin for the cold weather. He ate nothing but bread and beer. Friends noted that he was becoming pale and emaciated.

He finally died in 1686, at the age of 48.

ROBERT HOOKE
1635-1703

Robert Hooke toiled for several years in the Royal Society's laboratory, the deformed lab worker setting up experiments for wealthier gentlemen. However, the work he performed on the side to satisfy his own curiosity was consistently astonishing. He soon gained a reputation as one of the brightest minds in England.

In 1666, a catastrophic fire broke out that burned most of London to the ground. (It is now known as the Great Fire of London.) When it came time to rebuild the city, the king gave the job to Hooke.

Hooke's scientific work took a backseat as the rebuilding of London occupied all of his time. Despite the importance of his position, he never quite adjusted to his new status as a powerful gentleman. He lived a miserly life and became famous for dressing in shabby, tattered clothes. When he died, a chest was discovered underneath his bed that contained the equivalent of over a million dollars.

By the end of his life, not only had Hooke done groundbreaking work in astronomy, chemistry, physics, biology, geology, paleontology, and mechanical and civil engineering, but he also rebuilt one of the world's great cities from scratch.

You would think this would place him in the pantheon of great scientists, but over the next few centuries, his name essentially vanished from history.

It turns out that his personality was so prickly that the other members of the Royal Society (led by Sir Isaac Newton) buried Hooke's work. It is only in the last 25 years that Hooke's research has been rediscovered and his reputation restored.

WILLIAM "STRATA" SMITH
1769-1839

William Smith struggled with his upbringing his whole life. He was the orphaned son of a blacksmith, but he made himself into one of the most successful engineers in England. Despite this, he spent his whole life feeling like an outsider. He longed to be a true gentleman, a man of class and distinction.

In an attempt to join the upper class, he purchased a vast estate. However, the costs of running the estate and several bad investments sent him into bankruptcy. His home and property were seized by his creditors. He spent time in debtors' prison.

Humiliated, Smith picked up odd jobs whenever he could, and eventually settled outside London. However, in 1831, William Buckland urged the Geological Society to pay tribute to Smith's contributions to their field. They created an award to honor him—the Wollaston Medal, which is now considered the highest honor in geology.

Smith was never known for his humility, but he'd lived through enough unkind years to make him humble. At the award ceremony, he downplayed his own importance by telling the society, "Geology might have come along much faster if Newton had looked down at the ground instead of up at the apple."

GEORGES CUVIER
1769-1832

Like the dinosaur, Cuvier was the dominant figure of his time. With his incredible intellect and commanding personality, he ruled over Europe's scientific community for the first half of the nineteenth century. And like the dinosaurs, he was destroyed by something that came out of the blue.

On the Origin of Species, by Charles Darwin, was published in 1859, and it wiped out every idea that came before it. Evolution wasn't an entirely new idea. Various forms of it had been kicking around Europe for years (in fact, Darwin's own grandfather tinkered with the idea).

Cuvier, however, had found early versions of the theory laughable. He got into a famous debate with another French naturalist, who promoted an early (incorrect) form of evolutionary thinking. The debate spanned three months and took up eight separate meetings of the French scientific society. By then, the other members were bored of the subject, but Cuvier had the sort of personality that wasn't content until he had triumphed. He did.

After all, Cuvier built his fame around his uncanny ability to read the strata and fossil records, and what those said to him was very clear:

Life did not change a little bit at a

time. It changed through massive, great catastrophes ("revolutions of the globe"). Several times over the course of Earth's history, life as we know it stopped—

. . .

—and then restarted in a vastly different form.

Of course, this begged an important question: If all life was destroyed, then where did the next life-forms come from? On this, Cuvier was deliberately vague. Perhaps God created new animals, he said, or the disasters cleared the way for animals from other parts of the world to move in.

Darwin's theory, however, *did* answer the question. New animals don't magically appear. They survive, breed, and adapt to fit their new environment. The scientific community accepted the Darwinian revolution, and swept Cuvier's ideas into the dustbin of history. Like the dinosaur, his reputation was wiped out—

. . .

—only to be reborn.

In the past few decades, more and more evidence has emerged that supports Cuvier's idea of catastrophes. In the late 1970s, scientists found a massive meteor-impact crater on the Yucatán Peninsula of Mexico that corresponds to the same time that the dinosaurs went extinct.

Almost exactly 200 years after Cuvier predicted this sort of event, he was finally proven right.

But Darwin was right as well. In fact,

their theories work together.

The most accurate picture we have of Earth's past now tells us that life evolved slowly over billions of years, punctuated by five great extinction-level events: glaciers, oxygen depletion, volcanic eruptions, runaway global warming, an asteroid falling from space, and one that scientists still don't properly understand.

Whatever survived those events lived to see the dawn of a new era.

Cuvier's reputation is the perfect example.

MARY ANNING
1799–1847

Mary lived the rest of her life trapped between two worlds.

She had educated herself enough to know that she made some of the greatest discoveries in paleontology. She felt that she had outgrown Lyme Regis. "The society of her own rank is become distasteful to her," wrote a friend.

But she had nowhere to go. As a woman, she could not enter the world of science where she belonged. The night that Conybeare presented her plesiosaur to the Geological Society, Mary was not there. She only read about it weeks later in the society's journal. She would have noticed that despite discovering, excavating, cleaning, and illustrating the plesiosaur, her name wasn't mentioned once.

"The world has used me so unkindly,"

wrote Mary. A friend agreed: "These men of learning have sucked her brains, and made a great deal by publishing works . . . while she derived none of the advantages."

Despite these ill feelings, Mary continued to have a good working relationship with her childhood friend Henry Thomas de La Beche, and William Buckland, who greatly respected her opinion. Together, they made another fascinating discovery. After his Kirkdale Cave research, Mary knew that Buckland was fascinated by coprolites (fossilized poo). As she worked, she began to recognize coprolites *inside* the abdomen of several of her specimens (including the first plesiosaur).

When they cracked these coprolites open, they found the remains of the last meal that plesiosaur ate *200 million years ago*!

For several years, Mary made a comfortable living with her shop, but she was

Duria Antiquior by Henry de La Beche, 1830.

never far from money trouble. A dip in the economy hit the tourist industry in the 1830s and, once again, Mary had nowhere to turn. Fortunately, William Buckland and Henry Thomas de La Beche stepped in to help. Buckland convinced the British government and the Geological Society to award her small pensions that allowed her to live comfortably.

De La Beche, her friend from childhood, honored her in a different way. To raise money, he sold copies of an illustration he made that celebrated Mary's work. He combined her creatures (the ichthyosaur, the plesiosaur, the pterodactyl) with her discovery (the contents of their poo) and used Buckland's Kirkdale Cave methods to visualize a complete ecosystem. De La Beche called it *Duria Antiquior* ("Ancient Dorset"), and it is the *first image in history* that visualized what the Lost World looked like!

In the illustration you can see an ichthyosaur bite a plesiosaur that's so terrified it defecates as it dies; a plesiosaur plucks a pterosaur out of midair; a turtle eats a belemnite; a *Squaloraja* eats a lobster; and a bizarre-looking squid merrily flies about (it was actually an early guess at what an ammonite might look like out of its shell, with tentacles as sails!).

When Mary died of breast cancer at the age of 47, de La Beche read a brief eulogy of her at a meeting of the Geological Society. This was rarely done, and was considered a great honor. He said:

"Though not placed among even the easier classes of society, [Mary] had to earn her daily bread by her labour, yet contributed by her talents and untiring researches in no small degree to our knowledge. . . . The talents and good conduct of Mary Anning made her many friends. . . . She bore with fortitude the progress of a cancer on her breast, until she finally sunk beneath its ravages on the 9th of March, 1847."

That obituary was the only way she ever appeared inside the closed doors of the Geological Society. The society finally admitted its first female member in 1904.

GIDEON MANTELL
1790–1852

For most people, death is an end to their suffering. Not so with Gideon Mantell.

In the final years of his life, the pain from his carriage accident became so severe that he began taking large amounts of opiates (by the end, up to 32 times the recommended amount!). He eventually overdosed and died on November 10, 1852. That's when things got worse.

You may not be surprised to learn that the man responsible was Richard Owen.

A magazine published an anonymous obituary of Mantell that attacked his character. It described Mantell as a weak scientist, "in want of exact knowledge." It criticized his "overweening" ego. In the

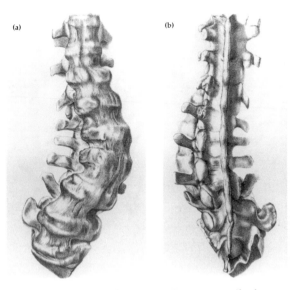

(a)   (b)

Gideon Mantell's spine twisted by scoliosis and a horse accident.

ultimate put-down, it even denied Mantell credit for the discovery of *Iguanodon*, giving the praise instead to Cuvier, Conybeare, and—you guessed it—Richard Owen.

But Owen wasn't done.

Mantell's spine was so twisted by scoliosis and his accident that the vertebrae were at 90-degree angles. Anatomists preserved it as an example of how badly the human spine can warp. They sent the spine to the Royal College of Surgeons, where it rested in a jar on a shelf under the watchful eye of the man in charge of the collection—Sir Richard Owen.

But Owen still wasn't done.

He was later put in charge of sorting the Natural History Museum's fossil collection. Not surprisingly, Mantell's contributions suffered the most. Owen sold and loaned out most of Mantell's pieces to other museums, ensuring that Mantell's lifework could never again be gathered in one place so that future generations could admire his remarkable achievements.

RICHARD OWEN
1804-1892

Science, and the advancement of knowledge, does not require a scientist to be good or evil. It only requires them to be right.

Being good, of course, is a far more pleasant way to deal with others. The same year that Owen wrote the Gideon Mantell obituary, he was due to become president of the Geological Society. However, the members had had enough of Owen's villainy. Due to his "pointed and repeated antagonism to Gideon Mantell," the other members voted against him.

Despite this snub, Owen's career continued to thrive. He received many more titles and awards. What ultimately ended his career was his inability to accept new discoveries. Just like Cuvier's, Owen's reputation did not survive the Darwinian revolution.

Owen was part of the old guard of the scientific community. He always tried to ground his discoveries in the context of the Bible and, to Owen, evolution and the Bible did not mix. In a now familiar pattern, he turned this basic philosophical

THE ANCIENT, AWESOME WORLD

Early illustrators of the ancient world envisioned it as a place of pure carnage, with terrifying beasts forever locked in a fight to the death. This is not, of course, how the natural world actually works (as anyone who has ever seen animals snoozing at a zoo can tell you).

Historians claim this misrepresentation is due to the fact that the first paleo-artists were scholars who spent their lives in cities. They were not tuned to the rhythms of the animal kingdom. Another, better explanation is that dinosaurs bring out the eight-year-old in all of us. Picturing them in battle is, quite simply, way more awesome.

disagreement into a heated rivalry.

He wrote articles and gave lectures savaging Darwin's research and intellect. The famously mellow, good-natured Darwin was taken aback: "He is mad with envy because my book is so talked about. It is painful to be hated in the intense degree with which Owen hates me."

Ironically, Owen's career perfectly illustrated Darwin's theory. The environment that Owen lived in changed (scientists adopted new ideas), but Owen could not adapt. So he went extinct. He was mocked. He lost elections to important posts. He lost jobs to younger colleagues.

By then, Owen was an old man. Forcibly removed from the front lines of research, he devoted the remaining years of his life into something remarkably noble—building a new home for London's Natural History Museum. Until then it had been a semiprivate institution, deliberately designed to keep away the riffraff. Owen wanted to build a grand new museum that was open to the public. In 1881, one of the great natural history museums in the world threw open its doors to all.

To honor Owen's accomplishments, a large statue of him was placed at the top of the main staircase in the great hall. A statue of Charles Darwin somehow wound up underneath the stairs . . . in the cafeteria. It was exactly how Owen always imagined himself—standing over the world of natural history like a god, his rivals pushed to the sides.

It stayed that way until 2009, the two-hundredth anniversary of the birth of Charles Darwin. To celebrate, the Natural History Museum replaced Owen's statue with the statue of Charles Darwin.

Owen is one of the most influential scientists in all of natural history, so his statue wasn't removed completely. It was simply relocated to a more out-of-the-way spot.

It's a funny thing. Science may not care whether someone is good or bad, but people do. When Darwin's anniversary passed, no one petitioned to move Owen's

Richard Owen is now under a set of stairs, little seen and ignored by passersby.

Charles Darwin gazing down from the top of the main staircase in London's Natural History Museum.

statue back. Darwin has remained at the top of the stairs ever since.

WILLIAM BUCKLAND
1784-1856

There is an old saying that "science advances one funeral at a time."

It means that scientists whose discoveries earn them fame and power tend to resist any new evidence that shows their discoveries were wrong. Progress only occurs after that scientist dies. Not so with William Buckland.

His cheery disposition and boundless enthusiasm for discovery left him open to anything. One evening, Buckland hosted a conversation with his brightest student, Charles Lyell. Over the course of the evening, Lyell picked apart Buckland's ideas point by point.

Buckland's reaction? He laughed heartily and confessed that Lyell might be right.

In the history of science, William Buckland is remembered fondly, but not with great respect. As a person, his decency and generosity is inspiring. He helped rescue both William Smith and Mary Anning when they were at their lowest. His colorful personality makes for good stories. However, what is remarkable about Buckland's later career is that he was confronted with the most difficult moment a scientist can face. He learned that he was wrong.

He'd spent his entire life trying to prove the existence of Noah's flood. He'd gathered countless bits of evidence and wrote best-selling books on the subject. But in 1838, a Swiss geologist named Louis

Agassiz invited Buckland to visit him in Switzerland.

Agassiz had a new theory—all of the "flood" evidence that Buckland gathered over his career (hills and valleys carved by larger forces) was actually the work of massive glaciers. Agassiz had discovered the Ice Age.

At first no one believed him. Buckland confessed that he traveled to Switzerland "with the determination of confounding and ridiculing [Agassiz]. But . . . he returned converted."

This was no small thing. The Bible said that Noah's flood was an act of God. Glaciers were not. The glacier theory meant that Earth was formed *without* God. Some of Buckland's closest friends weren't able to make the leap. Conybeare told him, "I don't quite believe in the former Geological supremacy of the Frost King."

Buckland began traveling around England, and as in the days of his youth, he saw the rocks and hills with new eyes. Science, he realized, was telling him a different story than what he had believed.

After two years of research and travel, Buckland cast aside every theory he'd worked on in his early career. He stood in front of the Geological Society and gave his full-hearted endorsement to the glacier theory. In typical Buckland fashion, he finished his speech with a dose of good humor. Anyone who didn't believe him, he said, "shall suffer the pains of eternal itch without the privilege of scratching."

It's hard to imagine how much courage this required. Buckland declared that he still believed in the biblical flood, but he had no proof of its existence, and it certainly was not responsible for the shaping of Earth.

This is a remarkable journey for one man to make over his lifetime. William Buckland was the son of a reverend, raised to believe in the Bible as the source of all truth. He spent his adult life believing in science's ability to find facts.

Unlike Owen, Buckland enthusiastically accepted and followed the evidence wherever it led him.

> Every time Buckland was given a choice between his beliefs (both personal and professional) and the observations of science, he chose science.

BILLY THE HYENA
1820–1846

After his time with the Buckland family, Billy returned to the care of his menagerie keeper in London.

The menagerie eventually closed, and Billy was moved to better living conditions at Surrey Zoological Gardens, a precursor to the London Zoo. On the journey to this new home, however, Billy managed to squeeze one more adventure into his eventful life. Billy and several deer escaped their transportation and spent an afternoon roaming the streets of London before they were captured. There are no reports about what sights Billy visited during his brief London holiday.

Billy eventually died on January 14, 1846. He was 26 years old, the oldest captive hyena in all of Europe.

MEGALOSAURUS
MIDDLE JURASSIC PERIOD
174 MILLION B.C.–EXTINCTION EVENT
(66 MILLION B.C.)

One of the strangest quirks of paleontology is that despite being the first dinosaur ever named, *Megalosaurus* remains one of the most mysterious. The assembled bones presented by Buckland all came from different individuals. No one has ever found a complete skeleton.

Over the next century, it became known as a "waste basket" species. Every time paleontologists found an unidentifiable fossil that belonged to a therapod (a carnivorous bipedal dinosaur), they would simply call it a *Megalosaurus*. However, as the fossil record expanded, scientists were better able to identify those other fossils with their appropriate species. Even the bones discovered by Gideon Mantell that were assumed to belong to *Megalosaurus* actually belonged to a different species, the *Baryonyx*.

Even now, almost 200 years later, the only true *Megalosaurus* bones that have been discovered are the handful dug up in Stonesfield, and a few others found in Wales. It is such a unique creature in history and anatomy that in 1827, Gideon Mantell honored its discovery, and the man who discovered it, by giving it the full scientific name of *Megalosaurus bucklandii*.

Those original fifteen bones from Stonesfield can still be seen (for free!) at Oxford University's spectacular Museum of Natural History.

THE CRYSTAL PALACE DINOSAURS
1854–PRESENT

The Crystal Palace remained popular for several decades after it opened. But as attendance slowly dwindled, the building began to deteriorate. In 1936, it burned down in a fire so large it could be seen from five different counties.

Thankfully, the Crystal Palace Dinosaurs escaped the flames. Over the next century, they kept a silent watch over their prehistoric park even as they were slowly forgotten. Trees grew over them. Their bodies began to fall into disrepair.

Recently, however, a group of enthusiasts known as Friends of the Crystal Palace

Dinosaurs (FCPD) lobbied the British government to fund the preservation of the dinosaurs as national landmarks. They succeeded, and received enough money to repair the dinosaurs and give them a fresh coat of paint.

Now the ancient creatures sit in the same quiet, tree-lined area of the park as they did in 1854. If you happen to be in London, you can even volunteer with the FCPD to help clean the dinosaurs so they look their best when they receive visitors from around the world. Or you can simply visit, like this author did, and see the spot where man and *Megalosaurus* first met face-to-face.

Author Ian Lendler and the Crystal Palace *Megalosaurus* meet for the first time. Despite the trick of perspective, the *Megalosaurus* is actually approx. 15 feet tall.

BIBLIOGRAPHY

Buckland, F. T., ed. *Memoir of the Very Rev. William Buckland*. London: George Routledge, 1858.

Buckland, William. Diaries and Lecture Notes of William Buckland. Oxford University Museum of Natural History Archives .

——. *Notice on the Megalosaurus or Great Fossil Lizard of Stonesfield*. Transactions of the Geological Society of London, 1824.

Cadbury, Deborah. *Terrible Lizard*. New York: Henry Holt, 2001.

Cutler, Alan. *The Seashell on the Mountaintop: A Story of Science, Sainthood, and the Humble Genius Who Discovered a New History of the Earth*. New York: Dutton, 2003.

Dean, Dennis R. *Gideon Mantell and the Discovery of Dinosaurs*. Cambridge: Cambridge University Press, 1999.

Emling, Shelley. *The Fossil Hunter: Dinosaurs, Evolution, and the Woman Whose Discoveries Changed the World*. New York: St. Martin's Griffin, 2011.

Gordon, Mrs. E. O., ed. *The Life and Correspondence of William Buckland*. London: John Murray, 1894.

Gould, Stephen J. *Eight Little Piggies: Reflections in Natural History*. New York: W.W. Norton, 1993.

——. *Time's Arrow, Time's Cycle: Myth and Metaphor in the Discovery of Geological Time*. Cambridge, MA: Harvard University Press, 1987.

Howlett, E. A., W. J. Kennedy, H. P. Powell, and H. S. Torrens. "New light on the history of *Megalosaurus*, the great lizard of Stonesfield." *Archives of Natural History* 44, no. 1, (2017): 82–102.

Lee, Mrs. R., ed. *Memoirs of Baron Cuvier*. London: Longmans and Co., 1833.

Mayor, Adrienne. *The First Fossil Hunters: Dinosaurs, Mammoths, and Myth in Greek and Roman Times*. Princeton, NJ: Princeton University Press, 2000.

McGowan, Christopher. *The Dragon Seekers: How an Extraordinary Circle of Fossilists Discovered the Dinosaurs and Paved the Way for Darwin*. New York: Perseus Books, 2001.

Oxford University Museum of Natural History website. "Learning more . . . geology." http://www.oum.ox.ac.uk/learning/geology.htm

Rudwick, Martin J. S. *Bursting the Limits of Time: The Reconstruction of Geohistory in the Age of Revolution.* Chicago: University of Chicago Press, 2005.

——. *Earth's Deep History: How It Was Discovered and Why It Matters.* Chicago: University of Chicago Press, 2014.

——. *Georges Cuvier, Fossil Bones, and Geological Catastrophes.* Chicago: University of Chicago Press, 1997.

——. *The Meaning of Fossils: Episodes in the History of Palaeontology.* Chicago: University of Chicago Press, 1976.

——. *Scenes from Deep Time: Early Pictorial Representations of the Prehistoric World.* Chicago: University of Chicago Press, 1992.

Scriven, Samuel. *Fossils of the Jurassic Coast.* East Lulworth, UK: Jurassic Coast Trust, 2016.

Winchester, Simon. *The Map That Changed the World: William Smith and the Birth of Modern Geology.* New York: HarperCollins, 2009.

ACKNOWLEDGMENTS

In the acknowledgment section at the end of a book, the author usually says something like, "I couldn't have written this book without these people." I don't think that's quite accurate. Without the following people and institutions, I *could* have written this book, but it would have been far less accurate, interesting, and entertaining.

This book, which is about the history of science, came to reflect the core values of science itself. Namely, the more information, peer review, and points of view I received, the better it became.

In particular, I would like to bow down in humble recognition of the incredible knowledge and generosity of Eliza Howlett, head of Earth Collections at Oxford University Natural History Museum, and Prof. Leonard Finkelman, paleontology and philosopher of science at Linfield College.

This book would not have been possible without Sir David Attenborough, who gave me the initial idea, or the two hardest working women in show business, Ruta Rimas and Nicole Fiorica.

I would also like to extend a huge thank-you to: the entire staff at the Axminster Heritage Center; Danielle Czerkaszyn; Kate Diston, head of Print and Digital Collections at Oxford University Natural History Museum; Jason Eaton; Deirdre Langeland (from my first book to my last); Chris Andrew, Richard Bull, and the entire staff at the wonderful Lyme Regis Museum; Tanya McKinnon; Dr. Ellinor Michel, chair of Friends of Crystal Palace Dinosaurs; Rebecca Stefoff; and the very great Dr. Ina Roy-Faderman.

Finally, and always, to Kusum.

CREDITS

Chapter opener collage art by Rebecca Syracuse

PROLOGUE

p. 4: *Scrotum humanum*. "The natural history of Oxford-shire : being an essay toward the natural history of England" by Robert Plot, courtesy of the Biodiversity Heritage Library

PART 1

p. 8: Engraved illustration of ancient warriors in battle. Bauhaus/iStock

p. 11: Mastodon skull. iStock

p. 12: Paper. iStock

p. 13: Book cover and interior fossil sketch. *The Natural History of Oxfordshire* by Robert Plot. Biodiversity Heritage Library

PART 2

p. 17: Galileo Galilei (1564–1642). Oil painting by an Italian painter, 18th century. Wellcome Collection

p. 18: Galileo with his telescope in the Piazza San Marco, Venice. Wood engraving. Wellcome Collection

p. 20–21: Benjamin Bell, System of surgery, 1801: surgical tools. Wellcome Collection

p. 21: Anatomy theater engraving by Willem Swanenburgh; drawing by Jan van 't Woudt (Johannes Woudanus). Public Domain

p. 21: Heart. iStock

p. 22: Book. iStock

p. 22: *Elementorum Myologiae Specimen Seu Musculi Descripto Geometrica*. Nicolaus Steno, 1667. iStock

p. 23: Sketch of *glossopetrae*. Wikimedia Commons/Public Domain

p. 24: Megalodon tooth comparison. iStock/Mark Kostich

p. 24: Ruler. iStock

p. 24: scuba Diver. iStock

p. 25: Crab fossil. Public Domain, courtesy of the Biodiversity Heritage Library

p. 27: Frame. iStock

p. 28: Microscope probably made by Zacharias Janssen; 17th century. Wellcome Collection

p. 28: Robert Hooke, *Micrographia*, detail: microscope. Wellcome Collection

p. 29: Ants. iStock

p. 29: Robert Hooke, *Micrographia*, head and eyes of drone-fly. Wellcome Collection

p. 29: Cover of *Micrographia*. Public Domain, courtesy of the British Library

p. 30: Robert Hooke, *Micrographia*, cork. Wellcome Collection

p. 30: Robert Hooke, *Micrographia*, fossilized wood. Wellcome Collection

p. 31: Brain. iStock

p. 32: Ammonite Fossil. Wikimedia Commons/James St. John

PART 3

p. 36: Tradescant House. This image was reproduced by kind permission of London Borough of Lambeth, Archives Department

p. 38: Tradescant the Elder. Wikimedia Commons/Public Domain, courtesy of the University of Toronto, Wenceslas Hollar Digital Collection

p. 38: John Tradescant II. Stipple engraving. Wellcome Collection

p. 39: Natural history museum of Ferrante Imperato of Naples. Wellcome Collection

p. 41: Elias Ashmole. Wikimedia Commons/Public Domain

p. 41: Hester Tradescant and stepchildren. Image © Ashmolean Museum, University of Oxford

p. 42–43: Ashmolean Museum, Oxford: the Clarendon Building. Line engraving by J. Le Keux, 1834, after F. Mackenzie. Wellcome Collection

p. 44: Duster. Public Domain

p. 45: Domenico Remps, Cabinet of Curiosities, Opificio delle pietre dure, Florence, Italy, Oil Painting, 1690s. Wikimedia Commons/Public Domain

of the South Downs. Illustration by Mary Mantell. Courtesy of the Biodiversity Heritage Library

p. 149: Charles Lyell. Library of Congress / Public Domain

p. 151: Iguanodon tooth. Ian Lendler

p. 151: Mary Mantell. © Oxford University Museum of Natural History

p. 156: Baron Georges Cuvier, holding a fish fossil. Wellcome Collection

p. 158: *Squaloraja* fossil. Biodiversity Heritage Library / JLR Agassiz's Recherches sur les Poissons Fossiles

p. 159: Autograph letter concerning the discovery of *Plesiosaurus*, from Mary Anning; sketch of *Plesiosaurus*. Wellcome Collection

PART 9

p. 162: Tickets. iStock

p. 163: Popcorn. iStock

p. 163: Plesiosaur fight. The British Library / Public Domain

p. 164: Plesiosaur and author. Ian Lendler

p. 167: *Megalosaurus* jawbone: © Oxford University Museum of Natural History

p. 168: Buckland family. Wikimedia Commons / Public Domain

PART 10

p. 172: Iguana. iStock

p. 173: The Royal College of Surgeons, Lincoln's Inn Fields, London: the interior of the Hunterian Museum. Colored engraving by E. Radclyffe after T. H. Shepherd. Wellcome Collection

p. 174: *Hylaeosaurus*. Wikimedia Commons / Public Domain

p. 175: Richard Owen. Wellcome Collection

p. 178: Richard Owen standing next to the skeleton of the *Dinornis maximus* (the extinct New Zealand moa). Photogravure, ca. 1877. Wellcome Collection

p. 184–185: Crystal Palace. Public Domain

p. 186: Steel engraving: Crystal Palace, 1851 exhibition. Wellcome Collection

p. 187: Gideon Mantell, sketch of *Iguanodon*. © Oxford University Museum of Natural History

p. 188: Gideon Algernon Mantell. Mezzotint by W. T. Davey after Sentier after J. Mayall. Wellcome Collection

p. 188: *Megalosaurus* jawbone. © Oxford University Museum of Natural History

p. 188: Hawkins's *Megalosaurus*. Ian Lendler

p. 189: Hawkins's studio. Wikimedia Commons / Public Domain

p. 190: Dinosaur Island *Iguanodons*. Ian Lendler

p. 191: Dinosaur Island. Ian Lendler

p. 192: Party invite. © Oxford University Museum of Natural History

p. 193: *Iguanodon* party. Illustrated London News / Victorian Picture Library

p. 194–195: The Crystal Palace from the Great Exhibition, installed at Sydenham: sculptures of prehistoric creatures in the foreground. Color Baxter-process print by G. Baxter, 1864(?). Wellcome Collection.

p. 196: *Bleak House* Cover. Wikimedia Commons / Library of Congress

EPILOGUE

p. 200: *Duria Antiquior*. Wikimedia Commons / Public Domain

p. 202: Mantell's spine. Hodgkin T, Adams W. Case of distortion of the spine with observations on rotation of the vertebrae as a complication of lateral curvature. Med Chir Trans 1854; 37: 167–80

p. 203: An ideal scene in the lower Cretaceous period in which an *Iguanodon* bites a *Megalosaurus*. Wood engraving by E. Ferington after E. Riou. Wellcome Collection

p. 204: Owen with bystander. Ian Lendler

p. 205: Darwin. Ian Lendler

p. 208: Ian Lendler and dinosaur. Photo by Theo Lendler

INDEX

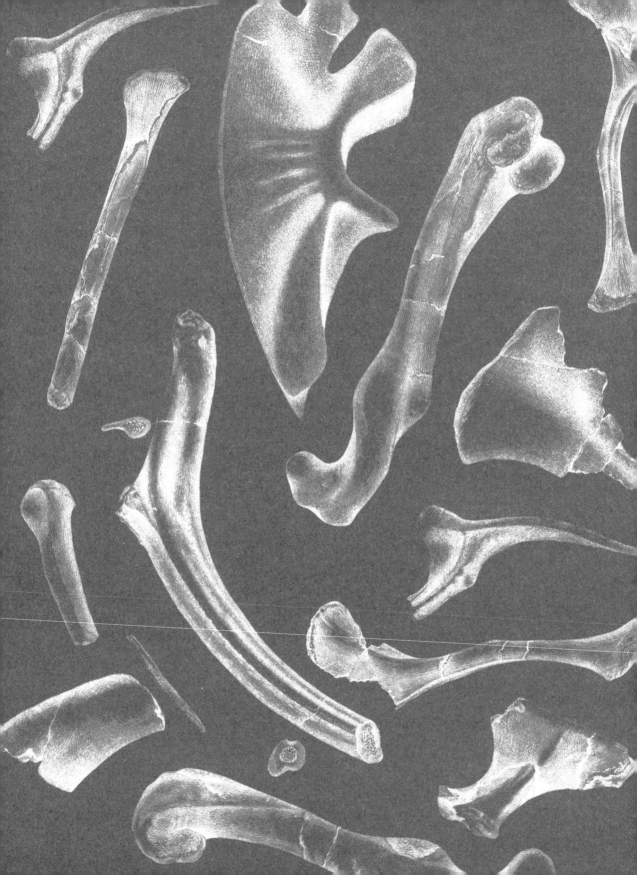